ASIAN AMERICANS

RECONCEPTUALIZING CULTURE, HISTORY, POLITICS

edited by

FRANKLIN NG
CALIFORNIA STATE UNIVERSITY,
FRESNO

A GARLAND SERIES

Asian Americans: Reconceptualizing Culture, History, Politics
Franklin Ng, series editor

DYNAMICS OF ETHNIC IDENTITY

THREE ASIAN AMERICAN COMMUNITIES IN PHILADELPHIA

JAE-HYUP LEE

GARLAND PUBLISHING, INC.
A MEMBER OF THE TAYLOR & FRANCIS GROUP
NEW YORK & LONDON / 1998

Library of Congress Cataloging-in-Publication Data

Lee, Jae-Hyup, 1966–
    Dynamics of ethnic identity : three Asian American commu-
nities in Philadelphia / Jae-Hyup Lee.
        p.   cm. — (Asian Americans)
    Revision of author's thesis (Ph. D.)—University of Pennsylva-
nia, 1994.
    Includes bibliographical references and index.
    ISBN 0-8153-3118-5 (alk. paper)
    1. Asian Americans—Pennsylvania—Philadelphia—Ethnic
identity. 2. Korean Americans—Pennsylvania—Philadelphia—
Ethnic identity. 3. Chinese Americans—Pennsylvania—Philadelphia—Ethnic identity. 4. Vietnamese Americans—Pennsylvania—
Philadelphia—Ethnic identity. 5. Philadelphia (Pa.)—Ethnic
relations. I. Title. II. Series.
F158.9.O6L44 1998
305.895073—dc21
                                                    98-27455

Printed on acid-free, 250-year-life paper
Manufactured in the United States of America

To Jisuk

Contents

Acknowledgments

This book began in 1993 as a doctoral dissertation. Melvyn Hammarberg, my thesis advisor, took earlier interest in the publication of my work. Without his generosity and encouragement, this book would not have been possible.

Numerous individuals helped me with this book in all the stages. My training in the Department of American Civilization at the University of Pennsylvania as well as in the Department of Anthropology at Seoul National University have set an important foundation for this research. Special thanks are due to Professors Margaret Mills, Jean Wu, Murray Murphey, Robert Schuyler, Kyung-Soo Chun, Sang-Bok Han, Kwang-Ok Kim, Kwang-Kyu Lee, Mun-Woong Lee, and Hahn-Sok Wang. At Northwestern University School of Law, Anthony D'Amato, Kenneth Abbott, Carole Silver, and Brian Williams helped broaden my perspective and develop a legal mind. I was also fortunate to have young Asian American attorneys as friends. I thank Simon Wong, Johann Lee, Joonmoo Lee, and Kyungwon Lee, who shared interests in my work and provided constant emotional support.

My deepest appreciation is credited to all of my informants in the Chinese, Korean, and Vietnamese American communities in Philadelphia for their kind cooperation which made my fieldwork so enjoyable and rewarding. I wish to express gratitude to Mr. Thomas Morton, Mr. Woon-Kin Chin, and Ms. My-Nhat Tran at Philadelphia Commission on Human Relations for assisting entry to different Asian American communities. I am grateful to number of peers who provided me valuable insights and constructive comments on earlier versions of this book: Beverly Butcher, Ellen Somekawa, Elise An, and Yuh Jiyeon. Dr. Bong Hak Hyun, Dr. Hie-Won Hann and reviewers and editors at Garland Publishing Inc. also provided thoughtful suggestions and expertise as I began the task of revision for publication.

I am indebted to a number of institutions for research opportunities and financial support: the University of Pennsylvania for the William Penn Fellowship from 1989 to 1994; the Balch Institute for Ethnic Studies for the exhibition project on Philadelphia Korean Americans from 1990 to 1991; and the Fabian/Baber Communications, Inc. for the film project on a Korean American family during the summer of 1993. Finally, the Department of English and the Graduate School of International Area Studies at Hankuk University of Foreign Studies provided important support. I especially thank my colleague, Dr. Alec Gordon, for his helpful comments.

Respectful appreciation is devoted to my parents who instilled in me the importance of education and have given emotional support when they were most needed. I also thank my brother and sister for their love and generosity.

I dedicate this book to my wife Jisuk Woo. I was fortunate to gain her intellectual support and companionship in such critical years of my life as a scholar and as a person. She has been a devoted friend and an outstanding critic since we first met at the University of Pennsylvania as graduate students. Although we took different intellectual paths and went to different law schools afterwards, we have finally become a family. It is hard to imagine writing this book without her very special kind of help. This book is hers as well.

JAE-HYUP LEE

Seoul, Korea

Tables

Dynamics of Ethnic Identity

1
Introduction

On a brief visit to Korea in 1990 after a year of graduate work in the United States, I visited one of my former professors. Upon hearing that I was studying Korean Americans, he said, "You didn't go all the way to America to study Koreans, did you?" To many Koreans and to some Americans as well, his question seems to be a valid one. Koreans living in a geographic area known as America are viewed by outsiders like my Korean professor as not being culturally legitimate Americans—whether or not they are legally Americans—since they have not been portrayed so. To these outsiders, America as a cultural entity is a hybrid of European civilization, thus to study American society or culture, one must start looking at "the Americans"—the White Anglo-Saxon Protestants.

I was not able to defend my position against my former professor at that time. My image of America and what it should look like, namely, that the American civilization started on the arrival of the early European explorers some 500 years ago, were not radically different from his. As an anthropologist, I came to the United States to learn about American society as an other culture. I expected America to be distinctively foreign and different from my Asian background. And indeed, Korean American experiences looked too familiar, and I positioned these Korean American experiences as a minor, or slightly insignificant one for explaining American social structure. I wanted to find an American cultural entity which I believed existed somewhere out there.

Then I started to realize that the white European majority and other racial and ethnic minorities have played equally critical roles in shaping American society. What we have in American history is a relationship between different racial and ethnic groups across time and in different social contexts. As a matter of fact, it is minority and ethnic experiences that can clearly illuminate the critical social relationships and the hidden organizing principles in American society. It was thus on the basis of this understanding that I decided to conduct research on Asian Americans because Asian American experiences can illustrate the interaction between the central concepts of American civilization such as race, ethnicity, gender, and class.

My brief visit to Japan in 1992 further stimulated my desire to compare different Asian American groups. Japan was the first Asian country that I have encountered, and I was surprised to find that so many things I previously regarded as distinctively Korean are also shared by Japanese culture. Japan seemed to be a good reference culture for a better understanding of Korean culture since, as an Asian, I could delineate the similarities and differences between the two countries. At the same time, my interpretation of Japanese culture would be quite different from that of non-Asians. If I were a person of European cultural background, I might end up describing cultural differences, many of which are Asian in origin, and are not particularly Japanese. I realized that in order to know each Asian American group better, it is necessary to compare those Asian groups rather than compare the group with the mainstream society. If we do not compare the Asian groups that comprise the umbrella term "Asian Americans," we tend to stress a lot of Asian characteristics which are common with those of white Americans, and thus are not able to address many aspects or problems pertaining to the particular groups.

Although Asian immigration to the United States began in the early 19th century, the Asian American experiences have not been well integrated into the scholarly discourse on race and ethnicity in the United States. Whereas the immigration policies have been reflected in the population, gender ratios, and employment profiles of Asian American communities, little attention has been paid to how U.S. immigration policy and law shaped the making of Asian America.

One common assumption about Asian Americans held by mainstream American society is the homogeneity among Asian groups. This assumed homogeneity is both physiological and cultural. Many non-Asians presume not only that all Asians look alike, but also that they think and behave in the same way. People seem to have very little knowledge of the histories and cultures of Asian Americans and very little awareness of the diversity among them. This ignorance leads non-Asians to lump all Asian Americans together and to perceive them through stereotypes. This lack of knowledge often leads to misunderstandings which ultimately contribute to anti-Asian sentiments.

Race, ethnicity, gender, and class have been important concepts for understanding social relations in American society, and have much to do with the making of social boundaries. Cultural categories along these four dimensions are used by groups to "cultivate differences" which themselves become institutionalized over time. A social boundary does not simply happen as a reaction of one dimension to another. It also reflects the traffic of symbolic meanings occurring within each of the systems or groups, in which the impact of external factors is refracted through the varied experiences of the members. For a more accurate assessment of the Asian community, therefore, we must first identify and acknowledge a variety of experiences across socio-cultural boundaries. In order to fully account for inter- and intra-ethnic relations, we must know how different members of an ethnic group manage to cope with their socio-economic environment. Only then can we assess the meanings regarding these differences and connect them in order to reconstruct our assumptions about the community.

Ethnicity is a pluralist, multidimensional, or multifaceted concept of self. Here I am mainly concerned with a fundamental—mutually and reciprocally defining—dialog of self and other. Various scholars have provided us with sophisticated understanding of hegemonic processes, analyzing how historical forces have constructed race, class, and gender. Poststructuralists like Derrida and Foucault, for instance, have highlighted how identity is defined relationally and how it is shaped by power relations among groups. Relations shape boundaries and categories. What we believe to be inherent cultural or social traits are in fact the results of the relations we have with others. As much as the nature of the group defines the relationship, the relationship also defines the nature of the group. The study of boundary making in general leads to a more sophisticated analysis of ethnic identity in contemporary America.

This book, therefore, is not concerned with whether primordial sentiments and moral cohesion are inherent properties of a "natural" ethnic community, but rather with determining the conditions under which a community becomes a meaningful social group. I have tried to depict how ethnic and class identities are constructed, and how distinguished identities are implemented or institutionalized through various networks and organizations. I have also analyzed how mainstream society, through its legal systems, has imposed a definition of identity on Asians in America.

The geographical area for this research is Philadelphia, but the problems and situations with which I am dealing will likely be similar to those in other metropolitan areas in the United States. I have focused on Korean, Chinese, and Vietnamese Americans since they comprise a majority of the Asian American population in Philadelphia. Since these three groups differ in terms of the context of migration and the degree of accommodation, comparison reveals the differences in their notion of ethnicity and community lives. However, my basic argument is that the external, politico-social impact of being a racial minority on their identity will be similar regardless of the ethnic or national background.

I hope this book will make a good case for the usefulness of microscopic description and analysis for understanding the nature of intergroup conflict and the relationship between politics and power, ethnicity and class. Examination of the structures and contents of personal networks illuminates both the processes by which social environments influence people and those by which individuals, in turn, act upon their social worlds. Hence, this book provides a conceptual link between individual and community, and thus micro and macro analysis.

This study also challenges various myths about Asian Americans prevalent in American society, such as the model minority thesis, their lack of political participation, and their silence in community activities.

By unraveling the complexity of the Asian American communities and the boundary strategies Asian Americans are using, this study provides a new view of the political processes which Asian Americans are creating in a variety of social settings. This study aims to be meaningful to the extent that it meets both practical needs and academic concerns by linking the everyday experience of ethnic group members with urban problems and public policy.

Part I deals with the theory and the historical background of this study. Part II provides descriptive analysis. The next chapter discusses the theoretical foundation of this research. It reviews major theories concerning American ethnic groups with special focus on the instrumental aspects of ethnic identity which is shaped and utilized by individuals and groups. The methodology and research procedure of this ethnographic study will be addressed in Chapter 3. The demographic and socioeconomic characteristics of interviewees are also included in that chapter. Chapter 4 briefly examines the immigration history of Chinese, Korean, and Vietnamese Americans, emphasizing the distinctive socioeconomic context these groups are introduced and its consequences for their immigrant experiences. Departing from the previous historical concerns, Chapter 5 mainly deals with the contemporary aspects of the research population in Philadelphia. A general overview of ethnic neighborhoods and the social components of each group are presented, along with some personal cases that illustrate these aspects. Chapters 6 and 7 discuss how individuals and groups in ethnic communities conceptualize ethnicity, and modify and reproduce it through numerous symbols and institutions. Comparison among three Asian American groups shows both inter- and intra-group variations. Chapter 8 will elucidate how mainstream society consistently impose definitions on Asian Americans, and how Asians defend or represent their identity against external constraints. Reviewing the diversity among Asian American communities, this research concludes with a discussion of ethnicity as relations, and provides some policy implications based on this perspective.

Part I Three Asian American Communities

2
Ethnicity: Basic Constructions

With the exception of American Indians, all American people are products of immigration. While most of the immigration has been voluntary, some of it, like that of African Americans has not. Regarding voluntary immigration, the great wave of European immigration which arrived from 1840 to World War I was the largest single immigration stream to the United States (Archdeacon 1983). At the same time, a major immigration wave from Asia began. China and Japan dominated the early immigration; more recently immigrants have come from Korea, Vietnam, and from other parts of Southeast Asia. In addition, there have also been very large influxes of immigrants from Canada, Mexico, the Caribbean, and Latin America.

Social scientists began to study immigration and the ethnic groups of the United States at the turn of the twentieth century. In particular a group of sociologists at the University of Chicago pioneered studies on urbanism and ethnic neighborhoods (Hannerz 1989). These Chicago ethnographers were interested in studying not the immigrants *per se*, but the integration process of immigrants into American mainstream society. The most prominent among this group of scholars was Robert Park and his theory of assimilation. According to Park, the contact among people would lead to a decline of initial cultural barriers, and thus eventually make immigrant cultures homogenized with and assimilated to the American mainstream culture. Park's view of the assimilation process was generally accepted by both lay people and professionals.

Based on this assimilation theory, the dominant paradigm for viewing American immigration history in the first half of the twentieth century has been the "melting pot" ideal. The original idea of the melting pot was the blending of all the component ethnic groups in America into a unique mixture. However, the melting pot idea in this sense has not been realized in practice. Much more common is what Gordon has termed "the Anglo conformity model" (Gordon 1964). According to this model, it is the English who immigrated first and established "the American culture" and all other groups have in time come to conform to the prevailing English or rather Anglo-American culture. The assumption that immigrants would eventually rid themselves of their foreign cultures and become indistinguishable from other Americans was widely held by the assimilationists.

However, beginning with the Civil Rights Movement in the late 1950s, the assimilation theory began to be challenged. The revival of ethnicity in the United States on a massive scale during this period came as a great shock to scholars and it showed that the melting pot thesis had to be revised. It turned out that there were many unassimilated ethnic groups and that bringing them into contact only increased their ethnicity rather than diminished it. Various studies have shown the enormous complexity of immigration phenomena. The assimilatory fate of immigrants into American society varies with their specific backgrounds in their country of origin, such as the characteristics of the particular place and time of immigration, and the degree of collective support. This series of events and studies suggest that the assimilation process has been much more complex than it was first generally assumed. Indeed, it turned out that the assimilation model has been altogether naive about the dynamics of the successful incorporation of immigrants into American society.

Research has shifted from assimilation to the dynamic process of ethnicization—driven, as it is, by multiple relationships—among various ethnicities as well as between them and the mainstream ethnicity. The critical questions being asked about are the very nature of ethnic identity. What is ethnicity? How is it related to immigration and how important is it? If the events of the 1960s show that the assimilationist view is inadequate, what view should be put in its place?

AMERICAN ETHNICITY: A THEORETICAL OVERVIEW

The new emphasis on ethnicity fastens on the ways in which groups and entities arise and define themselves against others. It also shows how external forces engage in the process of development and self-definition. Attention has been paid to how groups mobilize, shape, and reshape cultural repertoires and are in turn shaped by them. The dialectical process of identification includes how groups shape and reshape their self-images to elicit participation and commitment and are themselves shaped by these representations.

Given this new emphasis on theorizing ethnicity and ethnic relative, I will now consider different approaches to ethnic identity, and discuss multiple facets of the identity-making process.

The Primordialist versus Instrumentalist Debate

In discussing "ethnicity" or "ethnic identity," there have been two different approaches within social science scholarship which are often referred to as the "primordialist-instrumentalist" debate. Primordialists, view action as being value-oriented toward goals, while instrumentalists view action as rationally oriented. Primordialists tend to see ethnicity as a cultural or ascriptive notion. An ethnic group is defined as a collection of people who share a common culture of origin and heritage. Ethnic identity is thus based on "primordial sentiments," (Geertz 1962) that is, a more natural and involuntary phenomena. This cultural approach to ethnicity emphasizes cultural background and views the ethnic group as an "enclave," in which people maintain their unique culture and behavior. Its main research questions are focused on the continuation and maintenance of "tradition," rather than the dynamic mechanism of boundary maintenance.

On the other hand, instrumentalists emphasize that ethnic identity can be modified and reinterpreted by the individual members of an ethnic group, and even shaped differently (Barth 1969). Ethnicity is one of the political and economic resources which people use in a variety of social situations to accommodate their lives in a given society (Cohen 1981). The concept of "ethnic niche," derived from ecology, is thus useful for illuminating the interaction among ethnic groups as well as the interplay with the larger society. A critical issue which arises here is the processes of ethnic group formation and boundary maintenance.

The most significant example in recent American history is the massive ethnic mobilization since the 1960s. As has been already pointed out, the sudden resurgence of ethnicity in the 1960s, starting from the civil rights movement, called the traditional assimilation doctrine into question. What stands out from the 1960s experience is that people have multiple allegiances: religious, ethnic, political, class, regional, and occupational. People belong to many different social categories and groups, and they try to minimize conflicts among the allegiances they hold. According to the instrumentalist view, if all of the allegiances are not congruent, people choose to emphasize those allegiances which optimize their economic and social gains, and minimize those which jeopardize their survival probabilities. Put differently, ethnicity is a resource which people use to promote their well-being. Whether individuals will choose to emphasize ethnicity depends on the context in which they find themselves. For example, people will tend to downplay their ethnicity when they have more to gain by committing themselves in other allegiances.

The instrumental notion of ethnicity raises a number of important questions. How does the identity shared by members function within ethnic communities? Are there shared identities or simply the contention of multiple identities? How do members of an ethnic group define and relate to other ethnic groups? What are the dynamic mechanisms of maintaining ethnic distinctiveness in American society?

While the instrumentalist approach has inspired many scholars, the debate between primordialists and instrumentalists will not end. These two approaches do not have to exclude each other. Actually, culture and instrumentality feed on each other. Ethnic identity arises within the context of an available primordial identity which enables some kind of a visible instrumental advantage. What the primordialist and instrumentalist debate teaches us is that primordial sentiments and instrumentalist reasoning both play a part in determining people's conceptions of ethnic identity. They affect each other. Instrumental reasons can bring out long dormant primordial sentiments or push formerly prominent ones into the background, and these primordial sentiments can create perceived instrumental interests. Interestingly enough, tradition or culture itself has become more and more instrumentalistic and dynamic (Hobsbawm 1983), and the instrumentally manipulated traditions increasingly redefine primordial sentiments and meanings.

To shift our attention from the primordialist-instrumentalist debate, Gans (1992) broadly divides different approaches to American ethnicity into "straight line" versus "invention" theories. According to him, straight line theory looks at the American life of immigrants and their children from the perspective of the old country culture, and measures the way, extent, and speed with which they give up that culture. Conversely, invention theory looks at the process from the other end, focusing on what ethnic groups do now (Sollors 1989). Thus, the former under-emphasizes the present, and the latter under-emphasizes the past.

When ethnic symbols are considered to be revitalizing and reinventing, what matters is whether a group perceives the symbols as having ethnic significance in the process rather than the "genuineness" of the actual content of the symbols with reference to the . In other words, ethnic symbols need not have any conspicuous relation to the original culture. The cohesion of an ethnic community derives from an acceptance of a symbolic framework which can be shared by people with different interests and backgrounds. And the invention of ethnicity should be capacious and flexible enough to accommodate the variety of views which emerge from these differences.

The "invention of ethnicity" as a status category within American society occurs in a complex dialogue between American imposition of ethnic categories and the immigrant rallying of ethnic identities. It involves accepting ethnicity as a legitimate category of difference, and then attempting to shift its weighting, either for a specific group or for ethnic groups in general, from negative to positive.

Choice and Constraint

To illustrate how ethnic identity is constructed in the first place, scholars have paid attention to the two faces—individually defined and collectively constructed—of ethnicity. Ethnicity, first of all, is an individual identity. It is a matter of finding a voice or style that does not violate the several components of personal subjectivity. The search or struggle for a sense of ethnic identity is the (re)invention and discovery of a vision, both ethical and future-oriented (Fischer 1986). Sociologists' definitions of ethnicity stress that it involves the belief on the part of individual people that they are descended from a common ancestor and that they are part of a larger grouping. Fredrik Barth's (1969) contribution, for example, is to view ethnicity as a subjective process of group identification in which people use ethnic labels to define themselves and their interaction with others. Using his definition, the interactive situation is a major determinant of the level of inclusiveness employed in labeling self and others.

However, ethnicity also refers to group identity. Ethnicity opens up the question of categorization by non-members as opposed to an individual's identity or identification with a particular ethnic group. In other words, the definition of the ethnic identity of a group involves the members being identified and thus labeled by the surrounding society. Ethnic identification is, then, not so much a matter of individual choice as a constraint imposed by others. Although ethnicity has been more or less a matter of choice for white immigrants into America, as is illustrated by Waters (1990), this has not usually been the case for other races. Ethnicity is an easily definable identity—especially for visibly different minority groups like Asian Americans—and thus becomes a characteristic or feature beyond individual control. The concept of race itself is an extraordinarily obscure notion from the biological standpoint. It refers to the distinguishing physical features of people such as skin color, hair type, eye shape, etc. What counts is whether an individual's particular physical features are such that one is classified as a member of the racial group. As Omi and Winant (1994) aptly states, "although the concept of race invokes biologically based human characteristics, selection of these particular human features for purposes of racial signification is always and necessarily a social and historical process." In other words, race is really a social category, not a biological one.

In this sense "Asian American" is thus a racial as well as an ethnic term. As a member of a visible minority group, Asians have to deal with how others define them. The lives of racial minorities are strongly influenced by their racial or national origin regardless of how much they may choose not to identify themselves in ethnic or racial terms. When defining immigrants, what is stressed in the host society is not the individuality of the newcomers but their alien origin, the qualities they share with one another as "strangers." The charter group experiences consequently become crucial in defining the images and characteristics of immigrant groups. Hence, ethnicity is more than a matter of choice; it is rather a question of the defining power of constraints.

Ethnic Mobilization and Class

There has been a prevailing view that immigration is an individual phenomena, that immigrants decide to come or not to come to the United States as individuals. However, decisions leading to migration as well as the actual migration occurred in the context of chains of social networks, extending from the locality of origin to the destination. One of the most important changes in the analysis of American immigration has been the growing recognition of the importance of collectivism: the importance of the group, the family, the village, the ethnic enclave, and organizations, as opposed to the classic individualistic picture (Morawska 1990). Immigrants are not simply pushed out of their countries of origin, and many have brought resources from the group they left behind in their homelands. They then use resources that they have accumulated in the United States to help those who come after. The Chinese and Japanese who came to the West Coast depended on those who were already there for economic support. Immigrant organizations have developed to provide immigrants with credit, loans, and information. This collectivism was actually reinforced by American employers who often relied on ethnic-based hiring. Some employers directly imported groups of contract laborers as in the case of Japanese and Korean immigrants to Hawaiian plantations.

While studies of ethnic mobilization abound (Aldrich and Waldinger 1990; Bang 1983; Myers 1983), I will particularly point out that there are a variety of distinctions within ethnic groups. The French sociologist Pierre Bourdieu (1977) asserts that the most important tasks and status positions in society demand complex performances that can be mastered only by those who possess the necessary codes. These codes form the cultural capital of any society, a wealth that can be possessed only by those who have acquired the symbolic means to appropriate it. Cultural repertoires are differentially distributed within a culture-bearing population. Some symbolic codes and the ways of enacting them are monopolized by dominant elites through their privileged access to state and economic apparatuses. Other less-valued symbolic codes belong to groups of lower ranks and statuses, who also exercise less social power. Thus, there are ongoing struggles over the distribution and redistribution of these symbolic goods, and the results of these struggles have affected people's self-definitions (Wolf 1994). Bourdieu's "theory of practice" provides us with explanations for the differing cultural practices among ethnic groups based on the different modes of living, or "habitus" as Bourdieu terms them (Bentley 1987). According to Bourdieu, habitus is the site of the production of customs, strategies, interpretive skills, practical knowledge, and structured disposition, behind which lurk the "objective" social structures of the economy, politics, and kinship. It is a concept of great potential importance for understanding the construction of gender, ethnicity, and class in any society.

Using Bourdieu's theory of practice, Park (1991, 1997), in her study of Korean Americans in New York City, contends that the class affiliation within one ethnic group determined quite different ethnic experiences and conceptions. She argues that Koreans shape their ethnic identity by day-to-day ethnic encounters, with people constantly constructing and negotiating the realities based on their class affiliation within the Korean American community. In addition to the conception of ethnicity based on immigrant lives, other studies have found that there exists different viewpoints and different outlooks about immigrant life, as well as differences in the images perceived of the United States, which correlate with occupational and educational levels among Korean immigrants (Messaris and Woo 1991).

Gordon (1964) and Shibutani and Kwan (1965) demonstrated that people of different social classes tend to act differently and have different values even if they have the same ethnic background. Gordon's 'ethclass' is a useful concept for fusing both class and ethnic dimensions into a unified conceptual framework, by showing that race and class interact to produce different combinations of behavioral choices for ethnic groups at different levels of the status hierarchy.

Using statistical analysis based on path models, Jae Hong Park (1987) showed the persistence of class differences already formed in

Korea in Korean-American communities. Similarly, Shin and Han (1990) underscored the critical role of "internal structure," a resource shaped by immigrants' educational attainment and socioeconomic status, to the success of Korean-American small businesses. Yoon (1991) found the increasingly significant role of class interests and class resources rather than ethnic solidarity and ethnic resources in Korean small businesses in Chicago.

All of these studies demonstrate the importance of the class differentiation process in conceptualizing and mobilizing ethnicity and its resources. They reveal that each immigrant has his or her own social networks which appear more marked by class differentiation than by a common ethnic identity. Membership in the use of ethnic institutions and organizations are the devices which differentiate ethnic group members from each other as well as integrating ethnic groups based on a simple "ethnicity."

Institutions and Political Process

To illustrate how individuals relate to structure, scholars have paid attention to networks and institutions. The focus has been on the relationships within which people define and construct differences by demonstrating how ethnic institutions and organizations are the expressive mechanisms of differentiating ethnic group members from each other as well as integrating ethnic groups. As Giddens (1984) has reminded us, what must be grasped is not how structure determines action or how a combination of actions make up structure, but rather how action is structured in everyday contexts and how the structured features of action are thereby reproduced. Since social units of neighborhood, locality, occupation, and ethnicity are affected by and dependent on their participation in larger metropolitan, state, and interstate structures, ethnic groups must constantly strive to identify and validate the social boundaries which define them in order to survive as meaningful units of self-identification.

Legal anthropology (Moore 1978; Nader 1980) and Critical Legal Studies (Unger 1986; Tushnet 1991; Williams 1991) provide theoretical frameworks both for exploring how law acts to legitimize particular ideologies and asymmetrical power relations, and for analyzing the mutual construction of legal and social orders in historical time. According to their view, law plays a critical role in justifying and legitimizing the social order by inducing citizens to perceive the power of ruling groups as fair and acceptable. However, law confers legitimacy on the rules of dominant groups by obscuring real power relationships, making them appear to the mass of the population as reasonable and just. Habermas (1979) argues that the legitimacy of the modern state no longer rests on tradition or absolute values, but is instead rooted in conceptions of proper procedures deemed legitimate if they have been established according to norms of legality and constitutionality and if they conform to certain conceptions of citizenship and political representation.

Important aspects in regard to the relationship between law and identity-making are the ways law treats differences and boundaries between people and the assumptions which are built upon the legal analysis of such differences (Minow 1990, 1991). Historically the discrimination and violence against Asians in America has been systematic, legally legitimated, and officially institutionalized. For instance, behind many court rulings against the naturalization of Asians, there has been a common thread of racial legal reasoning stretching back to 1740 when the British Parliament passed the first law concerning naturalization in America (Lesser 1985).

However, at the same time, how people view the law is also a negotiated, constructed reality developed in local social settings through repeated interactions; it is not simply a faithful replica of the dominant ideology. In other words, in the bottom-up production of ideology, some aspects of the ideology of the dominant society are incorporated and others are not (Merry 1986). The important issues I am concerned with in connection with these studies are the limits within which these local ideologies are constructed and the implications of these constructions for maintenance or change in the existing social order in ethnic communities.

RESEARCH QUESTIONS

Ethnic identity is a multifaceted form of identity. It is a dynamic process, and each theory tends to focus on one aspect of its many faces. The conceptual framework of this study is that people are involved as active, creative participants in the process of constructing and negotiating coping and adaptive strategies. These strategies are "emergent" and "situational," in that they arise in a dynamic process in response to the needs and demands of the environment. The strategies of the group are marked by the cultural background and experiences of the group. An understanding of the coping, adaptive strategies of Asians must be understood as a dynamic interactive process in which situational and background factors take part.

Given the complex nature of ethnic identity, this study addresses the following questions: How and why are different boundaries (gender, national, cultural, or racial) important for different kinds of groups? I will compare Asian American experiences with those of white middle class Americans (for cross-reference on ethnicity among white Americans, see Alba 1990; Waters 1990). Are there important differences in the boundaries that are drawn by groups whose identities are defined by shared achieved characteristics (such as education or occupation) or, alternatively, by shared ascribed characteristics (such as race or gender)? Here I will examine to what extent categorization is manipulated instrumentally and how different boundaries interact with each other in this process at both the individual and group level. Are there variations in the boundary work produced by the members of different classes among Asian Americans? How do members of various social classes perceive the class system, their own status within the system, as well as their assessments of each other? What causes certain boundaries to be stable and used at home and in the workplace while others are influenced by other contextual factors? I will show how the differences of perception and interest between the members of ethnic communities are accommodated. In this way, I will try to find out how the personal choices of individuals are synthesized into an ongoing collectivity. I will look at the class composition and class politics within and beyond Asian American communities.

In particular, I will examine the intersection of various socially constructed boundaries, for example, those of ethnicity, gender, class and geographical locale. Asian Americans differ as to their average and range of occupational prestige and the degree of occupational specialization of group members. The orientation, cohesion, and structure of Asian American communities are reflections of a constant push and pull between the different views and stances of their members in the course of their manipulation of shared symbols. As Cohen (1985) notes, the community is "a cluster of symbolic and ideological map references within which the individual is socially oriented." The manner in which a person is marked depends entirely upon the specific community in question. The comparative analysis of the Chinese, Korean, and Vietnamese communities will provide valuable insights about how ethnic identities are practiced and manipulated differently.

My second emphasis will be to identify and illuminate the ways in which people shape their expressive behavior in relation to the conditions of their lives. In other words, I will look at how Chinese, Korean, and Vietnamese Americans experience the city of Philadelphia. I will thus ask: How do Asian Americans use expressive behavior to accommodate the new environment? How do they insert themselves into the larger power structures, or find ways in which to exercise choice and control? How can ethnic associations reveal the complex interplay of formal controls, tacit understandings and customs? What forms does (re)invention of tradition (Hobsbawm 1983) take in a heterogeneous and competitive urban setting? How do Asian immigrants in big cities form images of the larger whole and their place in it? What are the particular roles Asians play in the residential structure of cities and what is the impact of these roles on race relations? I expect that this close look at the urban life of Asian Americans will reveal the complex ways in which the traditionalizing process interacts with the defining features of urbanism as outlined by Wirth (1964).

Third, I will examine how mediating formal organizations are hierarchically organized and institutionalized, that is, have a structure that continues beyond the lives of those Asian Americans who are involved in them at any particular time. This focus on mediating institutions place issues of class and power at the center of the analysis. Mediating institutions—both government and private—shape, structure, and constrain interrelations. Change and transformation and processes of isolation or containment, as well as conflict, take place across boundaries or at their interface. For example, the governmental and quasi-governmental intervention of refugee resettlement plays a major role in shaping the urban experience of Southeast Asian refugees in Philadelphia (Somekawa 1992). Assimilation and change take place in the context of specific institutions where newcomers and established residents interact and have differential access to power. The contrast between newcomers and established residents allows us to focus not on ethnicity and issues of identity and assimilation but also on interrelations as they are enacted in particular situations and on strategies that produce a wide range of outcomes, from conflict to competition to accommodation.

Fourth, in a continuum of the analysis of mediating institutions, I will focus on how historical patterns, institutional barriers, and the economic forces of the wider society restrain or direct Asian immigrant experiences in inner-city localities. I will look at how individuals and sub-groups utilize their resources in the arena of politics. Among all strategies, electoral politics is only one activity pursued in order to protect and advance the interests of Asian Americans. The study of non-electoral activity will show how the Asian American experience differs from that of other immigrant and minority groups. Taking these non-electoral activities into account will enable us to understand the structural and legal barriers which prevented other forms of activity. Thus, I will include negotiations, demonstrations, and hearings into the category of politics as well as electoral politics. These research questions will illuminate the dynamic picture of the nature of ethnicity—choice and constraint—which I discussed earlier.

Finally, I intend to explore the extent to which legal ideology, as a system of categories and rules embodied within legal institutions, constrains and controls Asian Americans. I will also look at how Asian Americans creatively use the dominant ideologies and (re)construct the definitions of social reality to change and restructure the elements of the larger ideology. The legal disputes in which Asian Americans are engaged can be understood in terms of the cultural gap and structural differences these immigrant groups have to face. For comprehensive analysis, I will use the historical documents about court rulings as well as political and legal discourses in cases concerning Asian American issues. I will investigate the participants of competing interests who are involved in this process as important sources for illuminating the hegemonic dimensions of legal order. At the same time, I will examine letters written by readers to various local Asian American newspapers and see how ordinary Asian Americans handle self-defined issues and concerns and to what extent the dominant ideology is incorporated in this process.

SUMMARY

Through reviewing the existing literatures, we now have a better understanding of ethnicity, that is dynamic and interactional. Ethnic identity is one of several identities individuals conceptualize and negotiate throughout their lifetime. Ethnicity is a social construction, which stands in contrast with quests for an absolute, immutable and authentic ethnic identity independent of any particular social context. It has both primordial and instrumental dimensions in it. As an individual form of identity, the interpretation of ethnicity by members of ethnic group varies according to the several social categories they belong to. Through institutions and social networks, the different conceptualization of ethnicity is further mobilized and manipulated. As a collective form of identity, ethnicity involves the relations that each ethnic group has with other groups in a society, and the state that regulates it. Legal rules and categories, which reflect and impose majority definitions on social boundaries, can act as constraints on ethnic groups and thus become the ongoing battleground for the representation and negotiation of identities. With these research concerns in mind, let us move on to the next chapter, in which I will discuss the methodology used in this study.

3

The Process of Research

Information for this study was drawn from three different sources: fieldwork, which was conducted between 1990 and 1994; historical data and community documents including newspapers, brochures, booklets, and newsletters; and U.S. Census data. The legal and newspaper documents were collected through nationwide database services such as Dialog, LEXIS/NEXIS, and Ethnic Newswatch. The rationale for linking ethnographic research of present immigrant groups and the history of Asian Americans is that patterns in the history of Asians in America have an impact on their current arrangements. Thus I have attempted to discover the process of development of the Asian American community within the dynamic context of American society and culture in the light of the development of American urban areas. I intend to place these events in their relevant socio-economic and historical contexts in order to highlight dynamic processes rather than snapshot pictures. Emphasizing the historical, constructed quality of ethnicity implies an understanding of the ethnic group not as a thing, complete in itself and unchanging, but as a process that is characterized by the constant interaction of centripetal and centrifugal forces.

The empirical research undertaken takes the form of an ethnographic study of multiple generations in both urban and suburban settings within Chinese, Korean, and Vietnamese American communities. All the interviewees were current residents of the Greater Philadelphia area, and were at least permanent United States residents. Duration of residence in this area varied among interviewees. Some had directly arrived in Philadelphia from their country of origin, but others have lived in different parts of the United States. I limited my interviewees to Philadelphia residents because I believe there exist regional differences in ethnic experiences, and I wanted to control these effects.

It should be stressed that this study is exploratory in the sense that it attempts to reveal the diversity and interaction between and within each Asian American group, not to focus on one ethnic group. As outlined in the last chapter, it is guided by a number of major research questions (see Appendix for complete lists of questions). Answers to these questions have emerged from formal and informal interviews as well as from behavior observed during the interview.

In this book, the concept of community is not limited to a shared physical environment. It is applied to a symbolic level of community, including social network boundaries (Cohen 1985). For example, if people identify themselves as Chinese and participate in activities held in the Chinese American community, they are regarded as members of the Chinese community. The existence of the Asian American community is manifested by the occurrence of Asian activities or Asian gatherings in settings such as Asian homes, or buildings belonging to Asian organizations or rented from the immediate mainstream community and in the ethnic enclave. It is these settings, places, occasions, and activities that are taken to comprise the Asian American community.

ENTRY INTO THE FIELD OF STUDY

Ethnography is practiced through participant observation and in-depth description by anthropologists who are from outside the research community. Ethnographers, as professional strangers, approach their studies from the native's point of view. In other words, anthropologists have to maintain themselves as both insiders and outsiders at the same time. The task of maintaining the balance is difficult because fieldwork is based on different assumptions and perceptions of social reality between researcher and research subjects. Participant observation, or the fact of "being there," cannot ensure the authenticity of the anthropologist's analysis, and the authority based on knowledge produced as a result of empirical fieldwork methodology has been recently challenged (Clifford 1988). Ethnography is thus conceived as a reflexive process (Rabinow 1977), which involves the ongoing dialogue between the observer and the observed, both of who are equally defined by the context and relations of research and who are constantly engaging in the construction of social reality.

Being a Korean national, researching the Korean community in Philadelphia has been easier for me than studying the Chinese and Vietnamese community. Naturally I felt comfortable communicating in Korean with first generation Koreans, and most of the time I could relate to their viewpoints. I assumed that I already knew the rules and cultural meanings of the Korean American community. I soon found out, however, that the way I looked at and interpreted events and meanings in immigrant lives is based on a Korean perspective, an outsider view. I realized that the Korean American experiences and the cultures Korean immigrants practice are largely formulated or invented in the United States, and therefore viewing the Korean community as an extension of Korea often seemed irrelevant. The second generation, or 1.5 generation, was strikingly different in terms of their conception of Korean ethnicity, their outlook on American society, and the strategies they use to promote resources. In addition, my position as a Korean graduate student studying overseas or *Yoohaksaeng*, a highly regarded social status among Koreans, and my own upbringing in a middle-class family, were responsible for the cultural and socioeconomic assumptions which informed my initial approach. But, I am happy to say the fieldwork in the Korean American community in Philadelphia enlarged my perspective about what it means to be Korean.

In contrast with my taken-for-granted feeling of being at home with the Korean community, I entered the Chinese and Vietnamese communities very much as an outsider. I had never been exposed to other Asian communities except for occasional dinners in Chinatown. I have held a certain assumptions of Chinese and Vietnamese people. The only visible ethnic group in South Korea are 20,000 Chinese, and there has been minimal contact between Chinatown and the Korean mainstream society. Although Korea has been influenced by Chinese culture for a long time, I before conducting my research had not interacted with any Chinese people before. At the same time, my understanding of Vietnam was only shaped by one of my uncles who fought as a Korean soldier during the Vietnam War. In many Koreans' mind, Asia refers to East Asia, particularly China, Korea, and Japan. Vietnam is considered culturally different from the imagined Asia by many Koreans. However, the more I talked with people and learned from their experiences, I began to realize how similar their experiences are to those of Koreans. The values I previously thought to be distinctively Korean are also a part of Chinese and Vietnamese cultures. Working with other Asian American communities has enlarged my horizons concerning a variety of experiences and has caused me to think about many variables that account for making boundaries.

The interview segments presented in this book reveal insights about the immigrants themselves and the new land that has adopted them. The narratives of this presentation reveal a commentary, not only about their home country and Asian Americans, but about America as well. In a way, this is the way Asian Americans are positioning themselves in society, and it offers a critique of the current racial and ethnic relations.

My entry process to the Asian communities was like snowballing. Interviews with the Korean American community started in September 1990, and interviews with Chinese and Vietnamese Americans began in April 1993. The fieldwork in the Korean American community was conducted as a part of museum exhibition of Korean Americans in Philadelphia at the Balch Institute for Ethnic Studies. Through the contacts I made during this project, I was able to continue meeting people and participate in community activities. I started the interviews in the Chinese community with some members of the Holy Redeemer Catholic Church in Chinatown. I had initial difficulties interviewing Vietnamese people. Many of them were reluctant to be interviewed at first until they found out that I was a Korean graduate student. Some of them kept postponing previously scheduled interviews.

Interviews were conducted in the respondents' homes or offices and lasted between one and two hours. These interviews were held at times and places when the interviewees were available and where they felt comfortable. All of the interviews were audiotaped and later transcribed. All interview segments reflect words that were exactly spoken by the interviewees. Except for a few obvious inconsistent statements, minor grammatical errors were not edited. On a few occasions, some interviews were not taped if the informants were reluctant to be recorded. In that case, the transcription was based on my note-taking. After the initial formal interviews, some informants were selected for follow-up, focused interviews (as suggested by Spradley 1979). In addition to the formal interviews, I was invited to churches, social events, family gathering, parties, and holiday celebrations. These occasions provided opportunities for me to informally interview other extended family members and to observe family rituals and interactions.

INTERVIEWEES

A total of ninety-six interviews were conducted for this study (information about interviewees is given in the Appendix). Since the primary methodology for this study is qualitative and ethnographic, I have not attempted any statistical testing. I emphasize intensive, interpretative analysis rather than extensive, statistical approaches. The ethnographic method of capturing meanings from social action is the most useful tool for this study since I deal with a great degree of social complexity among Asian communities. As an ethnographer, I tried to understand people's perceptions of events and social relations and to clarify what the meanings are for the people involved in the events.

Any statistical assessment of my data would be biased. For one thing, the selection of informants in the Chinese and Vietnamese communities was limited by my inability to speak the Chinese and Vietnamese languages. Except for three informants, all of my Chinese and Vietnamese interviewees could communicate in English, although not fluently. Thus, they tended to be from the younger generation and more educated than the general population. In addition, the number of interviews with Chinese and Vietnamese was much smaller than those with Koreans. There were twice as many interviews with Koreans than with Chinese and Vietnamese. However, for an exploratory study, I believe that this sample size should be sufficient to provide an idea of the range and extent of different subgroups within the ethnic communities. Rather than statistically manipulating the data, I will show demographic and socioeconomic characteristics of my interviewees, and try to use this as a starting point for ethnographic analysis.

National Origin

I conducted 48 interviews with Koreans, 25 with Chinese, 20 with Vietnamese, and 3 interviews with non-Asians (two Caucasians and one African American) who have been close to Asian communities. Among the Chinese, in terms of the nationality before entering the United States, there are 11 from Taiwan, 8 from Hong Kong, 4 from Vietnam, 1 from Malaysia, and 1 from Mainland China (People's Republic of China). Including Chinese Vietnamese into the category of Chinese was somewhat controversial. Officially, they are counted as Vietnamese since they have been citizens of Vietnam. Many of them obtained refugee status in the United States just like many Vietnamese Americans. However, most Chinese from Vietnam identify themselves as Chinese. They had been a distinctive group back in Vietnam, and have maintained Chinese traditions since. Although their socioeconomic characteristics are more similar to Vietnamese than Chinese, culturally they are closer to Chinese. I put them into the Chinese category to see how they interact with both Chinese and Vietnamese communities.

In terms of nationality, the Korean and Vietnamese cases were pretty straightforward. All of the 48 Korean interviewees were from South Korea although some of them escaped as refugees from North Korea during the Korean War. Likewise, all of my 21 Vietnamese interviewees are from South Vietnam either before or after the Fall of Saigon.

Gender and Generation

Overall, with the exception of Vietnamese, male and female interviewees were evenly represented in my interview samples. My

Vietnamese informants were heavily oriented to male (15 vs. 5) compared to Chinese (12 vs. 13) and Korean (27 vs. 21) counterparts. Although I cannot argue that my sample represents the sex ratio in the Vietnamese American community in Philadelphia, I must point out that in general, the sex ratio among Vietnamese is more skewed toward the male than other Asian groups (Barringer, Gardner and Levin 1993).

In terms of generation, I define first generation as an immigrant, and the second generation as an American born citizen. I used the term "1.5 generation" to refer to persons who came to the United States at a young age, and attended at least American secondary school (Hurh 1990). They are generally bilingual or bicultural; however, some of my 1.5 generation interviewees were closer to the second generation in terms of upbringing. Among Chinese interviewees, 36 percent are first generation, 16 percent are second generation or beyond. First generation immigrants dominate among the Korean (80 percent) and Vietnamese (75 percent) samples. The percentage of 1.5 generation among my Chinese, Korean, and Vietnamese interviewees are, respectively, 48 percent, 16 percent, and 25 percent. This data shows that there is a high degree of generational diversity among Chinese Americans since they settled in this area well before the Koreans and Vietnamese.

Occupation and Education

In the United States, generally, occupation and educational level correlate with each other. However, in the case of many Asian Americans, this has not been always true. Their education level tends to be higher than occupation requires. Above all, the educational level of my sample is very high. For example, 60 percent of Korean interviewees and Vietnamese interviewees at least finished college. Forty-four percent of the Chinese interviewees received a college education.

My interviewees include a variety of occupations. Some of them are professionals, such as an architect, a doctor, an engineer, or an educator. People who own small business include discount stores, jewelry shops, deli owners, laundromats. My working-class interviewees were primarily employed in ethnic-owned businesses. Professional interviewees form 25 percent among Chinese, 23 percent among Koreans, and 40 percent among Vietnamese. Small business interviewees comprise 16 percent among Chinese, 40 percent among Koreans, and 25 percent among Vietnamese. The proportion of working-class people among the Chinese, Korean, and Vietnamese were, respectively, 10 percent, 10 percent, and 15 percent. The rest of the interviewee are primarily college students or the ones who have no current jobs.

SUMMARY

Qualitative analysis based on ethnographic interview and participant observation involves a constant interactions and dialogs between the researcher and the subject that is under study. The whole process is a reflexive and constitutive one, and thus it often leads to the debunking of prevailing stereotypes. For this matter, the ethnographic method used in this research can be a valuable tool to direct studies toward a better understanding of how people create or modify their collective representations and how traditional modes of representation might prompt or constrain these efforts at rendition.

The interviewees for this study were not randomly selected and cannot be used as accurate representation. However, some characteristics should be noted. According to my data, Chinese Americans are by far the most internally diversified group in terms of generation, country of origin, and occupation. Few generational differences have been observed among Korean Americans and Vietnamese Americans, and a significant number of Korean Americans are engaged in a small businesses. The intra- and inter-group variations among my interviewees in Philadelphia reflect the general pattern of Asian immigration and the socio-historical context in which the immigration occurred, as well as the policies that impact the population movements. I will discuss these aspects in a more detail in the following chapter.

4

Historical Aspects of Asian Americans

Immigration to the United States is not an isolated or peculiarly American phenomenon. With respect to the migrants' decision-making processes, immigration is an international system, and no part of the international migration system is entirely autonomous: each influences the others and is in turn affected by them, and all shape the choices migrants make (Barkan 1992). During the late 19th and the early 20th century, the development of industrial capitalism led to massive population shifts all around the world. The population movements first occurred in Northern and Western Europe, and then spread to Southern and Eastern Europe, and finally to the world at large. The population which came to the United States was a part of much larger world population movements that were set off by these economic changes. Immigrants, in other words, provided the labor supply for the development of industrial capitalism in the United States in the nineteenth century.

The Asian immigration to the United States is varied, not only in terms of the historical and cultural characteristics of its distinct nationalities but also with reference to the specific historical circumstances of immigration streams and the context in which immigrant groups are received. The flow of immigrants across the ocean has been altered by changing national boundaries and regimes, levels of economic development, and changes in American immigration policy. The different historical backgrounds and the specific contexts they came from are closely related to their preparation, motives, aspirations, and the prospects and outlooks toward the host society (Hing 1993).

Now, with these concerns in mind, let us turn to a brief historical overview of immigration history of the three Asian American groups. I will position Asian immigration in the broader structural changes in American society in terms of racial, social, and ethnic relations. First of all, let us look at the Census data to see the general trends of Asian immigration and its implication to the relationship with these groups. The following data shows the early Asian immigration to the United States until 1950, within which the Korean and Vietnamese were not yet categorized.

Table 1. Selected Asian Immigration Before 1950

	All Asia	China	Japan
pre-1850	232	46	N/A
1851-60	41,538	41,397	N/A
1861-70	64,759	64,301	186
1871-80	124,180	123,201	149
1881-90	69,942	61,711	2,270
1891-1900	74,862	14,799	25,942
1901-10	323,543	20,605	129,797
1911-20	247,236	21,278	83,837
1921-20	112,059	29,907	33,462
1931-40	16,081	4,928	1,948
1941-50	32,360	1,948	1,555

Source: Dinnerstein (1975)

As we see from the Table 1, the Asian population before 1850 was negligible. Chinese entered in great numbers from 1850 on, and their numbers peaked during 1870s. They were introduced into the United

States because of the labor demand for the rapid industrial development in the West, and they were consequently used to compete against freed black labor. Their fates were determined by racial and ethnic prejudice and public policy in American society. When their existence seemed to threaten local labor, Chinese immigration was suddenly stopped. The white laboring majority in California had obtained federal legislation that virtually cut off the flow of the Chinese immigrants in the hope of improving their competitive advantage on the labor market. The Chinese Exclusion Act of 1882 was the first proscription of an ethnic group in the United States (Dinnerstein 1975). Behind much of the anti-Chinese sentiment which ultimately led to this restrictive legislation was racism, the belief that there were vast cultural and racial differences between whites and Asians, and that the Asians are never assimilable.

The Japanese and the small number of Koreans formed the second wave of Asian immigration (Koreans were counted as Japanese since Korea was under the Japanese colonial rule at this period). As we see from Table 1, the number of Japanese increased dramatically after 1880 when the Chinese immigration stopped. The Japanese came to form an important proportion of the Hawaiian population as plantation laborers, but the American mainland eventually attracted the largest numbers of them. The success of the Japanese in California agriculture caused envy and hatred which were best expressed in the "yellow peril" scare just after 1900. Japanese immigrants surpassed the numbers of Chinese after 1890 and continued to dominate Asian immigration until 1924 when the Congress passed the Oriental Exclusion Act which halted virtually all immigration from Asia.

Discrimination and prejudice were common in most Asian American experiences until the end of World War II. Asians were officially denied citizenship by naturalization until the passage of the McCarran-Walter Act in 1952 which eliminated race as a bar to immigration and naturalization. Even the American-born Asian citizens were denied their basic civil rights during World War II. After the attack on Pearl Harbor, 120,000 Japanese Americans in California, two-thirds of whom were American-born citizens, were ordered to relocate themselves and were detained in concentration camps (Takaki 1989). Despite the government investigation (the Munson report) which undermined the assumed espionage and disloyalty of Japanese

Americans, the Japanese were nevertheless excluded from the definition of being American.

By the end of 1950, the largest Asian American groups were the Chinese and Japanese Americans. The composition of Asians in the United States, however, drastically changed in the latter half of the century. Some provisions in immigration legislation paved the way for new waves of Asian immigration. First of all, the Immigration Act of 1965 abolished the national origins quota system, allowing 170,000 persons to enter from the Eastern Hemisphere annually. For the first time, Congress placed a limit of 120,000 persons from the Western Hemisphere for fear of a massive increase in Latin American immigrants, especially Mexicans. The Immigration Act of 1965 also made possible more sympathetic regulations favoring the reunification of families and focused on specific labor skills or professional capabilities. However, the 1965 amendments were not originally intended to encourage Asian immigration. The family-preference system, one of the core parts in this legislation, was believed to insure that the new immigration pattern would not stray radically from the old one since it was assumed there were few Asian citizens who could sponsor their relatives and bring them to the United States (Dinnerstein 1975). However, a tremendous chain migration has occurred since then, and currently Asians make up half of the total number of immigrants to the United States.

The recent immigration from Asian countries has not only changed the ethnic landscape of American society but has drastically reshaped the composition of Asian communities in the United States. The influx of urban immigrants from Taiwan, Hong Kong, Korea, and India together with refugees from Vietnam, Cambodia, and Laos, have been so remarkable that the Chinese and Japanese are no longer in the majority among the Asian population. The Asian communities have been diversified in terms of national origin, and even divided along socioeconomic class lines. Given the overview of the history of Asian immigration into America, I will now move on to consider the immigration history of each Asian group and look at some important aspects of their experiences.

Chinese Americans

The Chinese have had a long history of migration to other countries. According to Chan (1991), many Chinese, especially from maritime regions like the Fujian (福建)and Guangdong (廣東) provinces and the island of Hainan (海南), started to move abroad. Their destinations included neighboring Southeast Asian countries, Hawaii, and the Americas.

The first wave of Chinese immigration to the United States occurred in the 1850s simultaneously with other immigration from Eastern and Southern Europe. They were pushed out by powerful forces at home as well as attracted by the discovery of gold and by jobs that became available as the American West developed. The introduction of Chinese was a part of the massive population movements into the United States which occurred when America underwent rapid industrialization and urbanization. Most of these early Chinese immigrants were from rural areas and were less educated.

When Chinese immigration was prohibited with the passage of the Chinese Exclusion Act in 1882, many Chinese in the United States went back to China. The Chinese who remained on the West Coast began to disperse throughout the country, relocating particularly to the East Coast which was more tolerant of them. Boston, New York, and Philadelphia were the cities which attracted many migrants.

One of the distinctive features of Chinese American experience is their forming of the residential or business districts, commonly known as "Chinatown" (Takaki 1989). Chinese immigration from the beginning involved the developing of strong networks. Information about a livelihood abroad from Western traders, travelers, ministers, and from immigrants themselves, was filtered through family and kinship networks to feed back to those who remained behind, and kinship networks helped pool the resources to facilitate the journey. Without extensive kinship networks that functioned as information providers as well as sources of support, the transpacific journey would not have been possible. Many Chinese immigrants resided where their families and kin members settled. In a way, the forming of Chinatown was a mechanism responsive to the host society. Isolation in Chinatown was both involuntary and voluntary. Racial resentment and discrimination forced them to stay together to develop their own community as a self-contained enclave, and to take up leftover work in the narrow margins of the larger economy. In addition, because of the need for social and cultural support from fellow Chinese, and the need to maintain ethnic identity and kinship ties with China, immigrants chose to reside in Chinatown because it reminded them of their home. Early Chinatown was a homogeneous enclave of bachelors, undifferentiated socially, economically, and geographically. Economic activities were often conducted within the family for basic sustenance.

Today's Chinatown, however, provides a different picture. The Chinese immigrants since 1965 originate from different parts of Mainland China, Taiwan, Hong Kong, and Southeast Asia. New immigrants possess varied levels of educational, occupational, and professional credentials and skills (Chen 1990). With the abolishment of Asian exclusion laws, the recent Chinese immigrants need not confine themselves to Chinatown, but they often suffer substantial downward mobility in occupation and social status in the larger labor market. Thus, regardless of their socio-economic background, they have still tended to cluster in Chinatown with their earlier counterparts. However, we should note that the new Chinatown is not merely a passive response to structural changes in the larger U.S. society. Rather, new Chinese immigrants have learned how to take advantage of their human capital and network of social relations to organize and develop economic opportunities within the ethnic community (Zhou 1992).

Korean Americans

Korean immigrants to the United States are part of more than five million Koreans living outside the Korean peninsula. The Korean influx into China has occurred throughout Korea's history because of its geographic proximity. Wars and starvation forced some Koreans near the border to seek land and flee from their situation to China. By 1907, the Korean population in Chientao (青島), Manchuria had reached 71,000 (Kim 1988). The growth of the Korean population in Manchuria increased drastically with the threat of Japanese annexation. At the same time, a sizable number of Koreans moved to Russia. When World War II ended, about 2 million Koreans were in Manchuria, and almost 1.8 million Koreans resided in China, the country with the largest Korean population outside the Korean peninsula.

A massive Korean influx into Japan occurred after the Japanese annexation of Korea in 1910. Under the National Manpower Mobilization Act in 1939 which established a Japanese colonial government, Korean laborers and military draftees were involuntarily brought to Japan, and about 650,000 Koreans are still living in Japan (Kim 1988).

The first wave of Korean immigration to the United States began in 1902 when a group of Korean people from different harbor cities around the Korean peninsula set sail for Hawaii as plantation workers (Choy 1979). American recruiters were eager to get manual labor from overseas, and they introduced Koreans as well as Japanese. Many of these early Korean immigrants were Christians. American missionaries who were active in many port cities around Korea during the early twentieth century played a significant role in promoting the Korean Christians' emigration to the "Christian God's Land" (Lee 1990). There was, however, an intermission of Korean immigration during the Japanese occupation of Korea between 1910 and 1945. The Korean War also had an impact on Korean society, and the penetration of American culture triggered more immigration. After the end of the Korean War in 1953, many Korean women entered the U.S. as wives of American soldiers.

The massive Korean immigration to the United States occurred after 1965. The immigration represents the period when the American economy began to shift from the labor industry into the service industry. In the 1960s and 1970s the world economy became increasingly globalized. As a result of America's involvement in the international market economy, a certain competitive sector in the United States was vulnerable to international competition. American capital helped to create the conditions for the immigration of cheap labor to the United States (Light and Bonacich 1988).

Emigration from South Korea to the United States, which began in the mid-1960s and grew to large proportions in the 1970s, was paralleled by a simultaneous growth in South Korean involvement in the world capitalist economy. In response to the increasing over-urbanization of Korean's industrial and commercial centers, the South Korean government actually encouraged emigration as part of its new population control program and as a means of maintaining economic stability. Thousands of young Koreans began to emigrate, particularly to West Germany, Brazil, Argentina, Canada, and the United States. The United States was one of the foremost nations active in bringing Korea into the orbit of world capitalism.

By nature, the Korean immigrants who came in this period are strikingly different from earlier Asian immigrants. They are mostly urbanites, sophisticated, pragmatic, more educated, and possess "cultural capital" (Bourdieu 1984) with an expectation of economic wealth and educational benefits. Subsequently, families of earlier immigrants entered the United States in great numbers. Korean Americans have become one of the fastest growing immigrant groups in the United States.

Unlike Chinese immigrants, Koreans do not have a resident ethnic enclave like Chinatown. They usually do not reside in Chinatown areas, either. Koreans do not tend to live in the same neighborhoods in which they work or set up their shops. Korean-run stores are often located in poor black neighborhoods throughout the city, but few Koreans reside in those areas. While some Korean businesses are for co-ethnics, most of their customers are Blacks and Hispanics.

Vietnamese Americans

Unlike the Chinese and Koreans, most Vietnamese in the United States are refugees, not immigrants. Immigrants choose to come to a new life, whereas refugees are forced to flee. The introduction of the Vietnamese to the United States was shaped by American military intervention in their country. Vietnamese refugees left their old life involuntarily because they were persecuted or feared being persecuted on account of their ethnic, religious, or political affiliations. While all immigrants face hardships upon arrival to a drastically different culture, refugees must also deal with the additional trauma of not being fully prepared to leave their native land, and therefore they often experience deep depression and frustration. Many Vietnamese boat people managed to land in Malaysia, Thailand, and Hong Kong, but only after watching fellow refugees die from hunger, thirst or exposure. Many others were killed, raped, robbed, brutally beaten and subjected to indignities by pirates (Takaki 1989).

The Republic of Vietnam fell to the control of the Vietnamese Communists in 1975 despite the intervention of the United States on behalf of the South. Hundred of thousands of people fled for fear of persecution by the Communist regime and sought asylum in the free world, especially in the United States, France, Canada, and Australia. That was the first time in the history of Vietnam that an exodus of such magnitude took place.

The first wave of Vietnamese refugees started coming to the United States after the fall of Saigon in 1975 with a mass exodus of the boat people from the shores of South Vietnam. The Vietnamese involved in the first wave were collectively well educated and wealthy in Vietnam. Having attended private, French schools, both men and women pursued advanced and professional qualifications.

The second wave occurred between 1979 and 1981. First, we need to understand the history of Chinese presence in Vietnam since many refugees from Vietnam during this period were ethnic Chinese. Chinese influence in Vietnamese culture has a long history although the Vietnamese people have kept their distinctive national identity. Vietnam has seen nearly ten centuries of Chinese rule, and subsequently became a tributary state. Population movements of considerable scale across the land border and waterways have been a familiar and recurrent phenomenon for centuries. The Chinese have come not only to dominate Vietnam's economy but also to be heavily concentrated in the largest city and commercial center of the country. It was assumed that at the time of Vietnam's independence in 1954 the Chinese controlled nearly 90 percent of all non-European capital investments in the country and enjoyed a near monopoly in a variety of wholesale and retail trades. Cholon, the heavily concentrated section of Chinese population ranked as the second largest Chinese city outside China with a population of 583,000 in 1951, next only to Singapore (Chang 1982).

After China invaded northern Vietnam in 1979, the Vietnamese authorities singled out the ethnic Chinese minority for particular pressure to emigrate. They loaded old freighters with thousands of ethnic Chinese, who had to pay in gold for their forced flight, and sent them out to sea. The arrival of these ships led to extended disputes between Western and Southeast Asian countries before the passengers were granted temporary asylum, usually in Malaysia. These refugees left with no possessions, but they had skills enabling survival in a foreign environment since many were merchants and manufacturers and therefore spoke several languages including Vietnamese and Cantonese.

Since the signing of a treaty between the United States and Vietnam in July 1989, under the "Orderly Departure Program," the third wave of Vietnamese has come to the United States. This immigration includes two specific groups: the Amerasian offspring of Americans in Vietnam, along with their family members, and former South Vietnamese officers and government officials who had been held as political prisoners. These former political detainees suffered mental abuse during their captivity and suffer post traumatic stress disorder which involves flashbacks, hallucinations, and extreme anxiety from the refugee experience.

The movement of Vietnamese to the United States has been one-sided whereas the interaction between Chinese and Korean diaspora and their homeland has steadily increased. However, the recent development of opening diplomatic channels between Vietnam and the United States will affect the fate of the Vietnamese community. Less than two weeks after the United States lifted its trade embargo on Vietnam in February 1994, the refugee group's steering committee ruled that, from then on, Vietnamese who flee would no longer be automatically entitled to consideration for a grant of asylum as political refugees but would be treated the same as asylum seekers from any other nation. This means that if the country where the migrants land rules that they are not refugees from persecution they can be sent home immediately (Kamm 1994). A growing number of Vietnamese entrepreneurs have been returning to their homeland to set up businesses. The dialog between Vietnam and Vietnamese American community will be expected to increase.

SUMMARY

Asian immigration to the United States is not new. The first wave of massive Chinese immigration dates back to the 19th century, and the Chinese, along with other European immigrants, were the active contributors to the development of American capitalist economy. However, most Asians were subject to racial prejudice, restrictive laws, and denied basic legal rights until the latter half of the 20th century.

The new wave of Asian immigration to the United States significantly altered the Asian American community. One of the newer immigrant groups, Korean Americans represent the "urban-to-urban" immigration with a great amount of cultural capital. Refugees from Southeast Asia have added another dimension to the already complex and diversified Asian American community. Each Asian group has come with different motives and aspirations, and each has different agendas and concerns. The next chapter will look at how these groups have experienced contemporary American society in general, and Philadelphia in particular.

5

The New Asian American Communities

ASIAN AMERICANS IN THE 1990S

The demographic and socioeconomic portrait of Asian Americans today reflects an extremely heterogeneous picture. Asian Americans are made up of physically and culturally diverse groups with different languages, customs, and values. Based on the 1990 United States Census, the estimated Asian and Pacific Islander population in the United States was 7 million, or about 3 percent of the nation's total. About 59 percent of all Asians and Pacific Islanders live in the western region of the United States. Regardless of regions, few Asians and Pacific Islanders (6 percent) live outside the metropolitan areas. Nearly all live in suburbs (49 percent) or central cities (45 percent). The median income of Asian and Pacific Islander families was $42,240 in 1990, compared with $36,910 for White families.

Although many people interpret this data to mean that Asians are successful, family income figures alone provide a misleading picture.

For example, the per capita income of the Asian and Pacific Islanders population ($13,420) was lower than that of the White population ($15,260). On average, Asians and Pacific Islanders have larger families and households than the White population, and this fact contributes to the lower per capita income figure. A larger proportion of Asian and Pacific Islander families (19 percent) had three or more earners per family than White families (14 percent). In addition, most Asians reside in major metropolitan cities where wages and living expenses are higher than the rest of the country (Cabezas and Kawaguchi 1988).

About 39 percent of Asians and Pacific Islanders aged 25 and over had completed four or more years of college in 1991, which was almost twice that of Whites at 22 percent. Despite the greater educational attainment levels of the Asian and Pacific Islander population, their median earnings were slightly lower than those of Whites both at the high school and college completion levels. To illustrate, Asians and Pacific Islanders who had completed high school and worked full-time, year-round had earnings of $19,290, compared with earnings of $22,050 for Whites with a similar education. The median earnings of Asians and Pacific Islanders at $34,470, with four or more years of college was comparable to Whites at $36,130.

When people claim that Asian Americans are socioeconomically successful, they assume that Asian Americans are more or less homogenous in socioeconomic status. However, the Asian and Pacific Islander population is very heterogeneous and the educational attainment varies considerably from group to group. There is a great difference between Japanese Americans who are not much different from whites, on the one hand, and the Vietnamese who appear more like Blacks and Hispanics on the other.

A larger proportion of Asian and Pacific Islander families (11 percent) than White families (8 percent) live in poverty. Even among Chinese and Koreans who all had higher median family incomes than the general population, the poverty rates are as high or higher than that of the general population, indicating the existence of significant class differences and subgroup differences. The national census data from 1980 and 1990 shows that the recent makeup of Asian American populations is very complex.

Table 2. Asian population by Groups 1980 and 1990

	Number (1,000) 1980	1990	Change, Number (1,000)	1980-90 % Increase
Asian/Pac. Islr	3,500	7,274	3,773	107.8
Chinese	806	1,645	839	104.1
Filipino	775	1,407	632	81.6
Japanese	701	848	147	20.9
Asian Indian	362	815	454	125.6
Korean	355	799	444	125.3
Vietnamese	262	615	353	134.8
Hawaiian	167	211	44	26.5

Source: Statistical Abstracts of the United States, 1993.

The 1990 Census indicates that approximately 23 percent are of Chinese origin, 12 percent are of Japanese origin, and 11 percent are of Korean origin, as well as 19 percent Filipino, 8 percent Vietnamese, 11 percent Asian Indian, and 16 percent Hawaiian, Pacific Islander or other Asian. Asian Indians, Koreans, and Vietnamese are the fastest growing groups in the Asian American population. Population increase among Japanese Americans has been minimal for the past few decades, whereas Chinese population steadily increased due to the new wave of immigrants from Hong Kong, Taiwan, and the Mainland. The regional concentration of Asian population varies according to groups.

Table 3. Percentage of Asian Persons by Group for the United States

	All Asians	Chinese	Korean	Vietnamese
California	39.6 (1)	42.8 (1)	32.5 (1)	45.6 (1)
New York	10.0 (2)	17.3 (2)	12.0 (2)	2.5 (8)
Hawaii	7.6 (3)	4.2 (3)	3.1 (10)	0.9 (20)
Texas	4.5 (4)	3.8 (4)	4.0 (5)	11.3 (2)
Illinois	4.1 (5)	3.0 (7)	5.2 (3)	1.7 (10)
New Jersey	3.9 (6)	3.6 (5)	4.8 (4)	1.2 (15)
Washington	2.8 (7)	2.1 (8)	3.7 (8)	3.0 (4)
Virginia	2.3 (8)	1.3 (12)	3.8 (6)	3.4 (3)
Florida	2.2 (9)	1.9 (9)	1.6 (13)	2.7 (6)
Massa.	2.1 (10)	3.3 (6)	1.5 (14)	2.5 (8)
Pennsylvania	2.0 (11)	1.8 (11)	3.4 (9)	2.6 (7)
Maryland	2.0 (11)	1.9 (9)	3.8 (6)	1.4 (13)

*Number in parenthesis is ranking.
Note: Other states of Korean concentration were Michigan (2.0
percent/11th), Georgia (1.9 percent/12th). For Vietnamese, they were
Louisiana (2.9 percent/5th), Minnesota (1.5 percent/11th), Oregon (1.5
percent/11th), Georgia (1.3 percent/14th), Colorado (1.2 percent/15th),
Oklahoma (1.2 percent/15th), Kansas (1.1 percent/18th), and Michigan (1.0
percent/19th).
Source: Statistical Abstracts of the United States, 1993.

As Table 3 shows, all three of the Asian groups reside
predominantly in the Western region. Most of them live in major
metropolitan cities around the country including Los Angeles, San
Francisco, New York, Honolulu, Houston, Seattle, Washington DC,
Boston, and Philadelphia. The Chinese, being the oldest among Asian
immigrants, follow roughly the general pattern of residence of all
Asians combined. Many of them concentrate in the areas where the old
Chinatowns were established such as California, Hawaii, and New
York.

However, Koreans have spread over different parts of the country,
unlike the Chinese and the Vietnamese. Their percentage of
concentration in California is the lowest among three groups, and
instead they are evenly distributed into major metropolitan cities

including Detroit and Atlanta. Unlike other Asians, Hawaii is not a major destination for Koreans. As I mentioned in the previous chapter, Koreans have more the characteristics of urban entrepreneurs than any other Asian group. The unusual attraction for the South appears to be attributable in part to a judgment that these areas present good economic opportunities.

The areas of concentration of the Vietnamese are very different from those of other Asian groups. Their destinations reflect the American resettlement policy of the Vietnamese refugees. Sponsorship requirements and the location of holding centers have contributed markedly to the geographic dispersion of Vietnamese Americans. Because of the magnitude of refugees and the absence of the established Vietnamese communities in this country, the United States government established four centers to house Vietnamese refugees while they waited for clearance to settle in a particular part of the country. California is the home of Travis Air Force Base, and Camp Pendleton, the nation's first and largest holding centers. Pennsylvania is the site of Fort Indiantown Gap, a holding center near Harrisburg that opened in 1975 (Fishman 1986).

In order to prevent large clusters of Vietnamese from building up in any given area, the government espoused a diaspora program which requires sponsorship. The diaspora policy through sponsorship created problems for the immigrants, for it caused the Vietnamese extended family to be broken up and resemble the more American, culturally acceptable, nuclear family. In reality this meant members of one family were separated from each other and were scattered throughout the country. Each refugee had to have a sponsor, and the sponsors were located near holding centers. Refugees passing through the resettlement centers usually remain in these states where they could most easily find sponsorships. More than 60 percent of Vietnamese Americans reside in California, Texas, and Washington combined. Quite contrary to the Chinese and Korean Americans, New York and Hawaii are not even included in the top five destinations for Vietnamese. The high rankings of Virginia, Louisiana, Florida, and some other midwestern states are the results of the resettlement programs. Pennsylvania ranks 7th among Vietnamese, 9th among Korean, and 11th among Chinese in regional concentration.

PHILADELPHIA: AN IMMIGRANT CITY

Philadelphia was a major industrializing center between 1830 and 1880, when large waves of British, Irish, and German immigrants entered. At the turn of the century between 1880 and 1920, like other industrial cities in the northeast, Philadelphia was a major destination for Southern and Eastern European immigrants. In the twentieth century, black immigration from the rural South was significant from 1930 to 1960. Each period of economic change is characterized by different patterns of immigration and spatial patterns of settlement. Each wave of newcomers entered a different opportunity structure in the labor and housing markets (Goode and Schneider 1994).

The postwar process of deindustrialization and the contemporary restructuring of the region's economy as a service economy make the city a very different context for the post-1965 wave of immigrants who have entered the United States. It transformed the demography of the city whose population became increasingly poorer and less white (Anderson 1990). Most of the White residents have moved to nearby suburban areas in Northeast Philadelphia. Today the city is half white and half black. Racial segregation has divided the city spatially.

The impact of the latest wave of immigrants has been relatively small in Philadelphia, largely because of the declining labor market and a poor opportunity structure. However, these new immigrants, mostly from Latin America, the Caribbean, and Asia, are arriving with much higher levels of education and a considerable amount of capital than earlier immigrants. The location of settlement is often newer suburban housing rather than the poorest housing.

The demographic characteristics of Asian Americans in Philadelphia based on the 1990 Census are as follows.

Table 4. Asian Persons by Group for Philadelphia

	City	Greater Philadelphia
All Asian	42,608 (100%)	80,282 (100%)
Korean	7,282 (17%)	17,985 (22%)
Chinese	11,414 (27%)	17,870 (22%)
Vietnamese	4,876 (11%)	7,961 (10%)

Note: Other sizable Asian groups in Greater Philadelphia area include Asian Indian (15,666), Filipino (7,947) and Cambodian (4,450).
Source: United States Census 1990, county by county illustration.

As we see from the Table 4, the Chinese, Korean, and Vietnamese population comprises 55 percent of the total Asian population in the city, and 54 percent in the Greater Philadelphia area. Although the proportion of concentration in the city among Asians (53%) is lower than Blacks (82%), it is much higher than Whites (30%). If we divide the Asian population into groups, the ratio is highest among the Chinese (64%), followed by the Vietnamese (61%), and Koreans (40%).[1] The existence of Chinatown and the Chinese residents linked with Chinatown's economy in the heart of Center City accounts for the concentration of Chinese. The relative absence of inner-city Korean ghettos are explained by the economic class of most Korean immigrants. Most Korean immigrants are young and educated, and from the urban elite or middle classes of South Korean society, and tend to rapidly move out to the suburbs. Resettlement housing for Vietnamese is located in West Philadelphia and South Philadelphia, and due to the relative lack of economic resources, many Vietnamese depend on public transportation and thus remain in the inner-city neighborhoods.

The Census data, however, usually tend to undercount the population. Calculation of population according to members of each ethnic community is much higher than official reports. Including city and suburban areas in Philadelphia, the estimated population by Korean, Chinese, and Vietnamese community are, respectively, 50,000, 30,000, and 15,000. I estimate that somewhere between the official report and unofficial calculation is reasonable.

ETHNIC NEIGHBORHOODS AND
SOCIOECONOMIC CHARACTERISTICS

The Asian American population is varied, not only in terms of the historical and cultural characteristics of its distinct nationalities but also in terms of the specific historical circumstances of immigration streams and the context in which immigrant groups are received. Given their very different histories of immigration and divergent rates of socioeconomic attainment, Asian groups display a wide variety of patterns and levels of segregation. Just as there is no such thing as an "Asian American," there is likewise no typical "Asian" pattern of segregation. Some nationwide surveys show that the ethnic segregation ratio among Asian Americans is generally high (Alba and Logan 1992; Massey and Denton 1992). The various Asian American groups have quite different levels of segregation. Moreover, the highest level of segregation between Asians of different levels of education or income is lower than the lowest level between Asians and whites of the same socioeconomic level, indicating that the residential segregation of Asians is not entirely a social class phenomenon (Barringer, Gardner and Levin 1993).

Chinese Americans

According to Chen (1992), the first Chinese arrived in Philadelphia in 1823. The first Chinese laundry shop was opened around 1870 at Race and 9th Streets, and the first restaurant was opened in 1880. The physical boundaries of Chinatown in Philadelphia were defined from the corner of 10th and Race Streets to 9th and Spring Streets. This location of Chinatown is regarded as overcrowded, unsanitary, and undesirable by outsiders, but it was nevertheless a valuable emotional outlet for the Chinese immigrants, providing them with comfort, safety, and symbols of the old way of life. Most of the Chinese in Philadelphia during this formative period were uneducated, non-English speaking laborers and lived in conditions of abject poverty. Although the Chinese population reached 1,000 by 1940, the Philadelphia Chinese community has not been a vibrant community due to the proximity of New York City, where the Chinese in Philadelphia depended on job opportunities and social services.

However, the Chinese in Philadelphia were not predominantly concentrated in Chinatown even in these early days. Only about one third of the Chinese population in Philadelphia was estimated to live in Chinatown in the early 1940s. The rest of the Chinese were living in North, West, and South Philadelphia. The early immigrants in the Philadelphia Chinese American community brought with them their native Cantonese dialects. During these early years, some Chinese schools were established. The first Chinese school started as a Chinese Sunday School around 1850 in Chinatown at the St. Andrew Church followed by the Chinese Christian Center and the Holy Redeemer Church on Vine and 9th Streets (Chen 1992).

Today, Chinatown has become a residential business district which clusters on Race street. The boundaries of Chinatown extend to Vine Street to the north, Arch Street to the south, 9th Street to the east, and 13th Street to the west. There are Chinese language captions on street signs to help Chinese residents who do not read English. Although the original Chinese settlers were primarily Cantonese, the current residents of Chinatown include people from Taiwan, Hong Kong, and different regional parts of mainland China, and Southeast Asia. Many Chinese immigrants dispersed from Chinatown, and some newer immigrants chose to live in the suburbs. Among the original Cantonese immigrants, the older generation stayed in Chinatown, whereas the younger generation left Chinatown searching for a better neighborhood and good school districts. Chinatown endures because as the second and third generations leave they are replaced by new immigrants. The different class backgrounds of the new immigrants have increased social stratification in the Chinese American community.

Many recent immigrants from Hong Kong or their families were originally mainlanders. Some left in the early 1950s to escape the Communist take-over, and some had illegally crossed the border in later years. They naturally flock to Chinatown, especially the ones who do not speak the language well. A lot of them started businesses in Chinatown and revitalized the Chinatown economy. The predominance of Cantonese can be illustrated by the fact that among the estimated 120 stores operating in Philadelphia's Chinatown, only four belong to Taiwanese owners. The others are either owners from Hong Kong, Vietnam, or older immigrants from Kuangtung. Immigrants after 1965 from Hong Kong also include managers and professionals. Recently, there has been a large exodus from Hong Kong because of Hong Kong's transfer to Chinese sovereignty in 1997.

Chinese immigrants from Taiwan are generally affluent, well educated, and skilled. They often take jobs in the mainstream American market. Some of them, however, decide to come back to start their own business such as lawyers' offices, realtor's offices, and architectural firms. These Chinese professionals sometimes realize that it is hard to break into mainstream society, and thus they decide to capture the ethnic market. Most of Taiwanese speak Mandarin and a Jujian dialect and carry a cultural tradition somewhat different from the Cantonese settlers in Chinatown. Because of these differences in socioeconomic background and culture, they tend to stay away from the Cantonese-dominated Chinatown. They often find many of the existing networks and organizations established by Cantonese not to be attractive or useful to them. They set up different organizations like the American Association for Ethnic Chinese as opposed to the Chinese Benevolent Association. There is also a minority population among the Chinese from Taiwan. This group of people who are Taiwanese natives before the establishment of Republic of China in the island of Taiwan are mostly concerned with the independence of Taiwan from the Republic of China.

Chinese people who live in the Center City, whether they reside in Chinatown or not, are all participants in the Chinatown networks. They work in environments that are predominantly Chinese, for example in Chinese restaurants, stores, and factories. They cannot afford to live in the suburban areas due to both financial and social constraints. They are most likely not proficient in English, to be recent immigrants, or have little education.

People who live in the suburbs also speak a variety of dialects, such as Mandarin, Taiwanese, Fuchou (福州), Hakka (客家), and Chaochou (潮州). A residential isolation along dialect lines is apparent. Many from Taiwan have immigrated after their study in the United States or have immigrated for investment or family reunification. They have higher levels of education and a higher socioeconomic status. Some Chinese schools and community associations are found in various suburbs such as Ambler, the Main Line, and Cherry Hill in southern New Jersey.

Since 1980, when Vietnamese refugees began to arrive in this area, some Chinese Vietnamese have opened their stores in Chinatown. The Chinese Vietnamese have tried to relate to the existing Chinese community because of their identification with resident Chinese Americans. However, Chinese from Vietnam were not immediately welcomed to participate in Philadelphia's Chinatown activities. Most of them speak both Cantonese and Vietnamese, and have set up their own organizations like the Overseas Chinese Association.

Korean Americans

The Korean immigration to Philadelphia began well before the first wave to Hawaii. Philip Jaisohn (*Suh Jai-pil*), one of the important Korean political figures during the Japanese colonization period (1910-1945), immigrated to Philadelphia, received a medical degree, and earned American citizenship. He was educated in Japan and later joined a political group called *Kaehwadang*, which staged an unsuccessful revolt against the conservative Korean government. As a result of the failure, he fled to the United Sates in 1885 where he continued his effort to liberate Korea from Japan (Liem 1984). Philip Jaisohn has become the symbol of Korean Americans in Philadelphia.

However, the massive immigration into this area in sizable numbers began after 1965. Even in the early 70s, the Korean community in Philadelphia was in a formative phase. At that time, there was only one Korean ethnic church in this area, and the Korean Association was formed by a handful of first generation Korean graduate students from Temple, Drexel, and the University of Pennsylvania. Many Korean immigrants during that period were professionals trained in the United States who entered the uppper middle class. During the 70s and 80s, however, the Korean population in Philadelphia increased dramatically.

Now more than 50,000 Koreans are believed to live in the Greater Philadelphia area. Koreans do not have an ethnic residential area like Chinatown, and they often soon move out to the suburbs. They use churches for regular meeting places and often establish a center for social and cultural gatherings. For Koreans, the major business districts are along North Fifth Street between Rockland Avenue and Cheltenham Avenue. The Olney area, where most Korean businesses are located, has long attracted aspiring middle-class population from further south in Philadelphia because of its newer and larger housing stock. When established whites began to move to the Northeast or the suburbs, they were replaced by Koreans, Latinos, and Asian Indians who are predominantly middle-class, and involved in small business, technical, or professional fields.

A major Koreatown on North 5th Street began in 1984 when the first Korean-owned pharmacy opened. Since then, Korean businesses have mushroomed in this area, and by the end of 1993, more than 130 Korean businesses had opened in this area. Especially on 5th Street between Olney Avenue and Godfrey Avenue, almost all stores are Korean-owned. They include all kinds of stores, such as travel agencies, groceries, jewelry stores, beauty salons, doctor's offices, lawyer's offices, real state agencies, bars, karaoke, and auto shops.

If you continue on 5th Street until the end, you will meet Cheltenham Avenue where a Korean shopping center is thriving. There is a Korean shopping center on Cheltenham Avenue which contains a large Korean grocery and about 20 other businesses such as a travel agency and a Korean Credit Union. This prospering shopping center, just north of the Philadelphia city limits, stands as a symbol of what has occurred in many suburban communities during the 1980s. Immigration has fed the growing Asian population, with many moving directly into the suburbs. At the same time, the white population has shown little growth.

In 1986, Koreans tried to put Korean language street signs on North 5th Street to bring some recognition to the growing Korean population of the neighborhood and to help elderly Koreans get around Olney. The signs along Olney's busy shopping strip were paid for by the Korean Association of Greater Philadelphia and were approved by city officials, but they were soon vandalized and destroyed by residents of the area. The incident, derived from residents' fear that the newcoming Koreans would take over the community, sparked serious debates about multiculturalism and brought local Korean merchants close to the established community in their own business interest.

Other areas of Korean business concentration are on 52nd Street in West Philadelphia, Germantown area, and recently in Upper Darby. While businesses located on North 5th Street aim at both Koreans and non-Koreans, those located in the West Philadelphia and Germantown areas are primarily targeting African American customers. Although

Koreans are well-known for their entrepreneurship in Black neighborhoods, they are not residentially integrated with Blacks. Their residential areas are more diverse. Most of them live in such suburban areas as Elkins Park, Broomall, and southern New Jersey.

Since most Koreans are from South Korea, there are few regional differences. In the Korean American's case, occupation and social class are the major indicators which define ethnic experiences. Since most of the Korean immigrants are from metropolitan areas in Korea and there are no distinctive social boundaries except class, the social stratification within this ethnic community is similar to that found in mainstream American society.

In the early 1960s, the South Korean government established overseas employment programs to send miners, construction and transportation workers, seamen and nurses to West Germany, Vietnam, and the Middle East to lessen the pressure of population growth as well as to acquire foreign exchange through emigrant remittances (Ishi 1988). At the same period in the United States, the Immigration and Naturalization Act of 1965 removed the barriers against immigration from Asian countries. The Act also allowed medical professionals to be exempt from the usual visa requirements of an employment offer and labor certification that there was insufficient manpower in the United States to perform the work. Koreans found entry into those sectors of the American medical system when and where there had been the most severe personnel shortages. In the growing health industry, the personnel shortages were on the professional levels of physicians, nurses, and technicians. This deficit was especially acute in government service: in urban hospitals, in state psychiatric hospitals, and in the Veterans Administration (Nishi and Wang 1985). Most of the Korean immigrants to Philadelphia during the 1950s and 1960s therefore were professionals, mostly doctors and nurses; immediately after 1965 especially there were massive movements among Korean medical doctors. As of 1985, of the total 1,057 graduates of the Yonsei medical college (one of the prestigious medical colleges in Korea) during the 1953-72 period, 442 were still residing in Korea, while 601 (more than half) were in the United States and fourteen were in other countries (Shin and Chang 1988).

On the other hand, recent Korean immigrants to the Philadelphia area, particularly during the 1980s, came from a variety of social layers. They come with different aspirations and often follow different economic strategies. They are different in terms of the historic roots of the regions they come from, and the economic careers they have pursued. This second group of people are working class. Mainly coming through their families' or relatives' invitation, these people usually lack enough money to start their own business, or skills to get into the major labor market. With the help of relatives and friends, they usually find information concerning job opportunities easily, but in relatively unfavorable workplaces.

Working class Korean Americans are employed in garment factories, laundromats, groceries, and discount stores. Some of them work in American factories, but others work under the supervision of fellow Koreans. It is reported that Korean store owners sometimes exploit these people with low wages. Working class Koreans usually work until late at night. As one of my informants who works at a Korean-owned discount store as a clerk told me, "some Korean supervisors demand more work of the recent immigrants than they did before they came." Working-class Korean Americans are acutely aware of the insecurity of their position, sometimes subordinated to both the enclave and the mainstream economy. However, these Koreans struggling with unstable employment and inadequate income are usually not exposed to the Korean community. Except for those who belong to a church, most working-class Korean Americans do not have enough time to join other organizational activities. The first five years—exactly the residence period required for U.S. citizenship—is very hard but most Koreans take it as necessary for them to be adjusted to the new environment.

The small business class comprises the majority of the Korean American population. Min (1991) reports that about 56 percent of recent Korean immigrants run small businesses. However, most of the business class never had the experience of running a store in their homeland. They are mostly from the middle class in Korea, and the education level among them is very high (college-graduated). It is seldom the case that the small business class moves into the professional class after immigration to the United States, whereas the reverse case is more prevalent. The business class acutely experiences downward mobility, and tends to strengthen their prestige by participating in the ethnic community. Serious competition among

Korean merchants is now the most important problem for them. Because of keen competition among the Korean small businessmen in the same line of business, almost all of the interviewees stated that they did not or could not receive any help from their fellow businessmen.

Vietnamese Americans

Many Vietnamese in Philadelphia began their life in the United States in Fort Indian Town Gap, later sponsored by the Nationalities Service Center, Hebrew Immigrant Assistant Service, Lutheran Family Services and Catholic Church World Services (Fishman 1986). The Vietnamese community of Philadelphia was a widely interconnected network of kin, friends, shops, and places to go that share a Vietnamese theme. The majority of the Vietnamese community were concentrated in several sections of Philadelphia: West Philadelphia, Southeast Philadelphia, Kensington, Hunting Park/Olney, and Logan, and recent development in Southeast Philadelphia on Woodland Avenue and in Upper Darby.

The biggest Vietnamese business centers are in South Philadelphia. About 3,000 Vietnamese are estimated to live in this area from 15th Street up to 18th Street, and between Wharton and Schneider Avenue. It is predominantly an Italian neighborhood with some Black sections. Many Vietnamese shops, restaurants and small businesses have sprung up in this Italian Market area in South Philadelphia. There are also some professional services, such as dentists and doctors' offices.

West Philadelphia is another pocket of Vietnamese residents. Because of the cheap housing in this area, resettlement agencies set up Vietnamese refugee population here. It has one of the more diverse populations in the city. Within this neighborhood, there are Blacks, Whites, Koreans, Japanese, Ethiopians, Haitians, Indians and Southeast Asian refugees. Recently, tensions have erupted between the Black students and the recently organized Southeast Asian refugee students, most notably in the University City High School in West Philadelphia (Peters 1988).

Other recent resettlements occurred in Northeastern part of Philadelphia: Hunting Park/Olney, Logan, and Kensington area. Hunting Park/Olney region is predominantly Black with some Hispanics. Socioeconomically, this area is more mixed, with sections ranging from the poor and devastated to middle class. Logan area is a predominantly Black neighborhood. While Kensington still retains some stable working-class families among both whites and Latinos, it has also become a locus of cheap rental housing and scattered-site public housing. It is in that context recent refugees were settled. Some Vietnamese small businesses opened in this area, such as grocery, restaurants, and jewelry shops.

About 2,000 Vietnamese live in the Upper Darby area now. Since this area is regarded as a safe neighborhood, many people move from South to Southwest Philadelphia once they obtain jobs. There are few Vietnamese-owned businesses in this area, and most of them work as janitors, and in clothing industries. Because residents in this area are relatively well-off compared to those of other areas, they can drive down to South Philadelphia to do their shopping.

There are not strong internal differentiations within the Vietnamese community in comparison with the Chinese and Korean communities. However, the year of immigration and the context in which they arrived are highly related to their experiences. Vietnamese who came right after 1975 when Saigon fell are mostly educated, but post-1980 Vietnamese are mostly refugee or boat people. Because of their relatively short immigration history, the existence of a second generation population is rare.

The elderly face many hardships in their adjustment to life in the U.S. They can be considered almost a "double-minority" since in addition to adjusting to a new environment like all immigrants, they also experience some isolation and loneliness than other citizens in this country experience. This limits their daily activities by preventing them from watching TV, speaking with neighbors (where it is customary in Vietnam to be well acquainted with the whole village), and visiting friends for fear of being stranded and unable to ask for help. In Vietnam the children usually provided transportation or run errands for their parents or grandparents but here the children are either at work or at school and are therefore unavailable.

Another important subgroup is the Amerasians. Since 1983, the United States has permitted these children of American fathers and Vietnamese mothers to apply to come to the United States as part of Vietnam's Orderly Departure Program. About one hundred Amerasian youth are estimated to live in Philadelphia (Peters 1988). While in Vietnam, they were believed to adapt to America quickly because of their American blood, but they are raised as Vietnamese with no difference to other Vietnamese youths.

ILLUSTRATION OF ETHNIC GROUPS

The Asian American community is heterogeneous, with peoples from all walks of life, a number of nations, ideologies, and sociocultural backgrounds. They are differently arranged in the city of Philadelphia. Here I will provide six cases of Asian Americans, two cases for each groups, to illustrate how diverse their background and their outlooks about American society are.

Case 1: Chinese from Hong Kong

Li-chiu[2] was born in Hong Kong. She came to the United States when she was 8 years old in 1976. When she first came to this country, there was no new housing in Philadelphia Chinatown. People could rent an apartment, but all housing was owned by Chinese residents in Chinatown. At that time, the Philadelphia Chinatown Development Corporation (PCDC) was accepting applications and providing people with information about availability in getting housing. Li-chiu's family applied for housing, and have lived in Chinatown since.

She has lived in one of the first housing units from the PCDC. Her grandparents have lived with her. They came to this country a couple of years earlier than she did. Before her family came to Philadelphia, Li-chiu's grandparents lived with her grandfather's aunt who has been living in Philadelphia Chinatown for 60 years. Her father arrived here first through the invitation of her grandmother. About 10 years after her father came to the United States, the rest of her family joined. Li-chiu currently has more than 50 relatives in Philadelphia.

When she first came to Philadelphia's Chinatown, most of Chinatown's residents had lived here for a long time, and there were not many immigrants. Chinatown was very quiet, and in no way as busy as today. People knew almost everybody in the street at that time. There was no big shopping center, only a few grocery stores, and restaurants were certainly not as many as there are now. The Imperial Inn and Ho Sai Gai were the only two restaurants people went to. Li-chiu has seen all of the new restaurants open one by one since then.

Case 2: Chinese from Vietnam

Margaret is an ethnic Chinese from Cholon, a heavily concentrated Chinese district in Vietnam. She left Vietnam in 1976 when she was 11 years old with her mother and younger sisters. Her family left in a boat. They first landed in a Malaysia refugee camp, and stayed there for three months. Her father joined them four years after Margaret's family settled down in Philadelphia.

Her father escaped a year after they did, and he stayed in Indonesia, then in Switzerland, and came over to Philadelphia, sponsored by the Nationalities Service Center. The latter set Margaret's family up in an apartment in the Logan area. Her family lived there for 7 months, and then settled in a row house. The government gave assistance for the first two years. Margaret's mother went to a cosmetology school, and opened a beauty salon in Chinatown in 1985.

Right now, Margaret lives in Pensauken, New Jersey. It is predominantly a Caucasian neighborhood. Since Margaret's mother is doing business in Chinatown, they have more contact with Chinese residents than neighbors in Cherry Hill. Margaret's father first worked at a restaurant in Chinatown. He did not speak English at all. He washed dishes first and later became a chef at the restaurant. Now he works as a chef at the Hyatt Hotel in Cherry Hill.

Margaret attended a Chinese school in Vietnam. She remembers that she took a couple of Vietnamese classes. She learned little Vietnamese since she did not have to speak the language there. Margaret spoke English a little bit when she came to the United States because she had learned English with a tutor. Life in Cholon was pretty insulated since all of her friends in Vietnam were Chinese. Her grandparents do not even speak Vietnamese although they have lived in Vietnam for almost 50 years. She thinks that the older generation Chinese often look down on the Vietnamese, and are so stubborn that they would not attempt to learn Vietnamese. Margaret's family brought many relatives after they settled in Philadelphia. They sponsored Margaret's mother's brother from a refugee camp. He currently works at a Chinese restaurant in downtown, and his wife makes clothes at home.

Margaret identifies herself as Chinese, or as Chinese from Vietnam. She feels that most Chinese in Chinatown have an assumption about the Chinese from Vietnam. Chinese residents seem to think that the Chinese from Vietnam are lower than them. She thinks the Vietnamese and the Chinese Vietnamese relate better here in the United States since they came from the same country.

Margaret's first boyfriend was a Caucasian. They had a long relationship for four years. Her father was really against the relationship, so they eventually broke up. When she went out with a Chinese guy, her parents were very happy about it. She once dated a Filipino man, and her parents did not approve of the relationship. They clearly seem to prefer a Chinese for her mate.

Margaret encountered many stereotypes about Asians. Many Americans assume that all Asians are very smart, especially in math. Because Margaret is terrible at math, she surprises her teachers and friends. She is upset at the fact that boys are more respected in her family. Her brother never washes dishes. Her mother understands that Margaret has helped a lot with her business, but she still holds the traditional value of preferring males.

Margaret's best friend now is Korean. For some reasons, she does not have a lot of Chinese-Chinese friends. She feels more comfortable being with Asians, not particularly with Chinese. At home, Margaret eats Chinese foods regularly. Her mother keeps to the family traditions. She celebrates holidays such as Chinese New Year's Day and Moon Festival. Margaret understands the meanings of holidays, but she does not really care about them.

Every Mondays and Wednesdays, Margaret works with her mother all day for 8 hours. Then she goes home, studies, or watches TV. On Tuesdays and Thursdays, she spends time in school, and studies at the library. On Fridays, she goes to the internship. On weekends, she works for her mother all day. She belongs to the stamp collecting club at Temple University. She thinks that education is very important for her to become successful. She does not think the bachelor's degree can get her anywhere. She wants to pursue at least a master's degree.

Case 3: Korean Small Business Owner

Mr. Park came to the United States in 1985 with $3,000 in hand, which he describes as "bare hands." He dreamed of becoming a millionaire, but life in the United States was not as easy as he expected. He started a variety discount store. Within two months after his arrival in

Philadelphia, from the time his brother came to Philadelphia 5 years ago, he searched for a business opportunity with him. One day he found an empty store, and he thought it promising, so he took the store with borrowed money from *kye* (Korean rotating credit association). *Kye* is a very important financial resource for Korean businessmen like Mr. Park. Like other Korean store owners, it was the only source of finance available for him. Fortunately, the business was successful so that he could soon pay off the debt. After he ran the store for one year, he sold it to another Korean, and moved on to a Korean video rental business. However, he failed in the business within 3 months. After he lost all of his money, it became much harder to start from the beginning. Mr. Park worked as a part-time manual laborer. After he earned some money from work, he opened a clothing store again with the help of *kye* money.

What Mr. Park regards as a big problem among Korean business owners now is the severe competition among Korean co-ethnics. Due to the competition among themselves, Korean businessmen have to offer price reduction and some incentive bonuses to customers, and thus end up hurting each other.

Mr. Park now owns a store in a White neighborhood. In his judgment, most Americans see Koreans as just plain Asians, or as Chinese. He is very upset to be called a Chinese. In terms of inter-racial relationships, he thinks most Koreans look down on Blacks even though most of them own businesses in Black neighborhoods. Blacks in turn look down on Koreans too, he believes. From the businessmen's standpoint, he feels Hispanics are better customers. One of Mr. Park's friends is running a business in a 100 percent Hispanic neighborhood, and he thinks fewer conflicts exists there than in Black neighborhoods. According to him, the Vietnamese are now doing business in locations where Koreans first started business. Because Koreans fought during the Vietnam War and helped the Vietnamese people, he thinks Koreans are somehow better than the Vietnamese.

When Mr. Park has medical problems, he always goes to a Korean doctor at the Philip Jaisohn Medical Foundation. However, he prefers to retain an American lawyer. He once lost a case where a Korean lawyer represented him. He thinks Korean lawyers are not so powerful because the American power structure is White-oriented. Therefore, to him, it is much easier to find a well-known American lawyer and win the case.

Mr. Park became a sincere Christian after he arrived in America. The Korean American community is church-centered, so all of the information and social gatherings are from the church. He observes that among those Koreans who go to church, half are very sincere Christians, but the other half go to church for social reasons. Currently, he does not belong to organizations other than church and *kye*.

Even though his wife is an American citizen, Mr. Park does not intend to obtain U.S. citizenship at the moment as he is not sure of whether he should live in Korea or in the United States in the future. Although Mr. Park thinks he can make more money in America than in Korea, he does not think life in the States is any better than life in Korea. During the 1980s and 1990s Korea has rapidly developed economically, and he hopes to return to Korea someday.

Mr. Park has a rather unique view about educating his children. He wants his children to be whatever they wish to be. But he hopes one of his two sons will study further and the other will become a military officer. In America everything seems so liberal and disordered to him. He got furious when he heard that most American kids have their first sexual experience at 13 or 14 years of age. Because Mr. Park wants to isolate his kids from this "polluted society," he wants his eldest son to go into the military. He thinks the military culture is better than the secular culture.

Case 4: Korean 1.5 Generation

(Note: Although this Korean teenager is not one of my interviewees, I found this autobiographical article from *Philadelphia Woman*, the journal of the Korean Woman's Association written in Korean, quite insightful about the problems of 1.5 generation Koreans).

I came to the United States when I was young with my mom. I went to an American school because I was told to do so. I remember the first day I went to school. I looked around the classroom over and over, but there was no one like me [Korean]. I could not understand what the teacher said, nor could I comprehend what kids around me were telling me. I could not even figure out what was written in the blackboard.

Most of the times, I returned home right after school without saying a word in English. I felt really sad at home.

I thought life in the United States would be wonderful. That's what everybody said in Korea. I missed my friends in Korea. When I was in Korea, I was very popular, but here, I could not even go out and hang around the streets.

Since I was lonely, I wanted to be always at home with mom. One day, she gave me the keys of the apartment and said, "Now, I have to go out and make money. I'll make a lot of money, then we can buy a car. I will be able to buy you delicious foods. You understand?" Then she showed me how to unlock the door. And then she said, "Don't go outside. Those Black guys will kidnap you. You come home immediately after school!"

I was frightened. I was happy and safe at home with my mom, and since she is not here any more what can I do from now on? When I imagine that I have to be home alone, I began to become panic. I cried, "Mom, I am scared. I don't want to be alone." She scolded me saying, "You're a boy. You should not be such a sissy." And then she fell asleep. She would not even talk with me any more.

At school, what I liked most was lunch time. I could eat ice cream, pizza, but soon I got tired of them. I always ate alone at the corner, and kids would throw things at me, calling me "Chink." I came home with great anger, but I put up with it. I wanted to talk to mom about it and cry, but all I saw after school was the empty house. I could not stand it any more. I ran outside. I was somewhat relieved by the fresh air. I walked around the street cautiously, and it was not as bad as mom said.

I liked walking around the street. It was better than staying at home alone. I was no longer scared. I could forget about what happened in school. In the meantime, I managed to make friends in my neighborhood. I was really pleased to know somebody, since I had no friends at all. After school, I would hang around with those guys until my mom got home. I was really happy with them. No fear at all. My friends would protect me, and I needed nothing if I was with them. I began to feel happy about being in the United States for the first time. Years have passed, and I became a high school student. I grew taller than my mom.

Then my mom became such a nuisance. "Study hard. Did you finish homework?" "All of your cousins got into good colleges, but how come you don't do well in school?" "I came to this country and worked my fingers to the bone only for your well-being, and you don't appreciate that?" Mom and I did not communicate well. It was always a one-way conversation.

Mom soon found out that I was playing hooky. She received a report from school, and she got angry. She told me that she would leave me and go back to Korea, and then she disappeared. It was terrible! Without mom, cooking was a big problem. I ate instant noodles every day, and then I ate meals in my friends' houses. I often skipped meals. During that time, mom telephoned me occasionally. I promised her that I wouldn't be absent at school any more, and then she came back. I wanted to study hard, listen to my mom, but I couldn't stand it. Whenever I was at my desk, I had a headache. I finally started playing hooky again.

Mom was so disappointed at me, and she moved me into a different school. I wanted to concentrate in the new school. But I was a stranger in that school. Nothing came into my mind while sitting alone in the classroom. I missed my friends in the old neighborhood. I went back to visit my old friends, but I felt that I did not belong there any more. I could not finish high school after all. I regret that I came to the United States. I missed Korea, my home. If only I had stayed in Korea . . . Where do I have to go now?

Case 5: Vietnamese Restaurant Owner

Mr. Pham was born and lived in a coastal city not far from Saigon. Originally, all of his family had been Buddhists. However, his grandmother suddenly became Catholic, and his mother-in-law followed, so he became Catholic. But Mr. Pham himself seldom went to church. When he was six years old living in a highland of Vietnam, he hated to climb the mountain to attend the church for a daily mass with his mother. After those experiences, he does not go to church regularly.

Mr. Pham is an ethnic Vietnamese, but he has a Chinese wife. Marriages between Vietnamese men and Chinese women were not easy in Vietnam. In the beginning of the nineteenth century, many Chinese men moved around to earn money, married Vietnamese women, and then brought them to mainland China or left them in Vietnam because their first wife was usually in mainland China. But Vietnamese men

could not marry Chinese women because of the assumed superiority by
the Chinese. Marrying a Vietnamese man was considered a step-down
in the social ladder. However, Mr. Pham had a high position in a big
pharmacy company, and he used his position as a regional director to
convince her family for a long time.

When Saigon collapsed in 1975, Mr. Pham could not escape
Vietnam immediately. Being a well-to-do manager, all of his property
was confiscated by the Communists. The Communist government did
not allow him to continue his work, so Mr. Pham had to open a fish
pond to raise fish. Sooner or later he organized a boat to escape
Vietnam, with 56 people along with his family. Most of people in the
boat were his friends. Mr. Pham brought 9 members of his family; his
wife, mother-in-law, and five children and a cousin. After seven days,
he and others were rescued by a Japanese shipping liner. He stayed in
Japan for 11 months before he came to the United States. That was the
first time he had ever been to a foreign country. The experience opened
his eyes and stimulated him to learn more about other Asians. Mr.
Pham was quite impressed by the discipline of Japanese people. In
Japan, all high school students wear uniforms, and that kind of
discipline, he thought, is responsible for the economic success of Japan.
He also respects Koreans who fought during the Vietnam War. He
remembers three Korean military divisions that were sent to help South
Vietnam: the White Horse, the Blue Dragon, and the Tiger. He was
impressed how disciplined and tough those Korean soldiers were when
they were at battle with the North Vietnamese.

Since Mr. Pham worked at a pharmaceutical company before 1975,
he have made a lot of friends from the American Army and the Navy.
One of them sponsored his family to come to the United States. When
Mr. Pham first came to the United States, he first worked for a
wholesale pharmaceutical company in Hartford, Connecticut, for two
years. Although he could write in English fairly well, thanks to the
second language education in a high school in Vietnam, his spoken
English was not good. So he started as a manual laborer at the
company. The work was really hard. It required a shift work, and he
sometimes had to work from 10 PM to 8 AM in the morning. One day,
Mr. Pham visited one of his friends in Philadelphia, who was a
Vietnamese doctor. His friend showed him a restaurant located in South
Philadelphia which the owner wanted to sell at that time. He took over

the restaurant in 1980. At the time Mr. Pham purchased the restaurant, the owner gave a credit because the business was so slow. And he opened and soon paid back the money he owed.

Mr. Pham lived from 1980 to 1983 in South Philadelphia, then he moved to Roxborough, 25 minutes from the restaurant he now owns. Roxborough is a working class neighborhood. Only a couple of Vietnamese families and some Korean people live in the same neighborhood. Mr. Pham's restaurant work is from 11 a.m. to 12 midnight. But when he arrived here and opened the restaurant, he sometimes worked until 2 am on Fridays or Saturdays. All of his family members work at the restaurant. For 7 years, they did not take any vacation at all. They regarded freedom to be expensive.

Mr. Pham's family speak Vietnamese and Cantonese at home. They live in a multicultural and multilingual environment. Because his mother-in-law is a Cantonese, she communicates with granddaughters in Cantonese. Mr. Pham himself can speak Cantonese, Vietnamese, English, and French. His first daughter can speak Vietnamese, Cantonese, Mandarin, English, and Spanish. All of his daughters can speak at least Cantonese, Vietnamese, and English, and they study Mandarin once a week. His first daughter graduated from a pharmacy school four years ago. The second daughter has graduated from a business school, and took a job at an accounting firm. The third and fourth daughters are first-year students in a pharmacy school. The last one is a first year student in college. Mr. Pham has an interesting viewpoint about instilling cultural values. Three of his daughters attended a Karate club. Mr. Pham wanted to teach his children the philosophy of the martial arts to keep them disciplined.

Mr. Pham visits Washington DC, New York, Connecticut and meets friends, talking together and sharing experiences about how to deal with generation problems, how to raise children and so on. He does not work on any Vietnamese organizations because he does not find time. But many Vietnamese visit him and ask him how to apply for a driver's license.

As an American citizen, Mr. Pham votes regularly. At the presidential election in 1992, he bet $700 on Clinton. At that time, he thought Americans would vote for Clinton, because the economy was so bad and people wanted a change. With respect to interaction with Americans, Mr. Pham is mostly bothered by the misconception here that the Vietnamese get money from government. He sincerely told one customer that he opened his business because he worked for 16 hours a day, and accumulated money step by step. His family did not buy many clothes, and received no government money.

In 1990, he went back to Vietnam with some American friends as a translator. On that occasion, he had a chance to visit his hometown, because his mother passed away in 1989. Since he was the only son, he very much regretted when she passed away in his absence. He plans to go back to Vietnam someday. At his age, he thinks living in Vietnam is better than living in the United States. He expects a lot from the recent normalization between the United States and Vietnam.

Case 6: Vietnamese Political Prisoner

Lately, there has been a wave of political refugees, who served in the South Vietnamese government before 1975, and most of them had been in concentration camps for at least three years. These people have tremendous emotional scars, and when they came over to the United States, they hope the United States government will reimburse whatever loss they had in 15 years. However, they were treated just like other refugees, and they were very upset about it.

Mr. Phung Tran is one of this group of people. He was born in 1939. He began his teaching career from 1961 until 1966 when he was drafted into the military. He went to an officer training school about 30 kilometers from Saigon. He spent about five months there before he was sent to the United States for further training from 1967 to 1968 at Fort Maine in Georgia. After graduation, Mr. Tran went back to Vietnam, and became a training officer at the non-commission officer academy, and worked there for two years. Then he was transferred to a language school in Saigon to teach English to those officers who wanted to go to the United States. In 1972, he was sent to the United States for the second time. At this time, he was to be trained to become an English teaching officer. Then he went back to Vietnam and became a captain in the Army. Mr. Tran could not escape the country when South Vietnam fell. He had to stay with his family, and the Communist government put him in prison. They put all of those who were closely related to Americans or former regimes into so-called "re-education camps." It was the worst time of his life. He remembers those years in the camps as being very tough, bitter ones. He spent five years in prison. The communists took him to the North. They did not let him stay in the South. He had to live in the mountainous areas, in jungles, where he was brainwashed and put to hard labor.

Finally, Mr. Tran was released in 1980, and joined his family. Without him, his family had a hard time to make a living. He could not immediately resume teaching, but few years later, he could run small private classes. At first he had some difficulties in getting students since the government banned teaching English.

Under the HO Program which is exclusively reserved for former officers or other people who are related to the United States government or South Vietnam government, he came to the United States. All of his family came to the United States with a short intermission in Bangkok for four days. He joined his brother who was already living in Philadelphia. His brother also had to spend 6 years in prison like him. He was released one year after Mr. Tran was released. However, in 1981, his brother, together with his wife and two children, escaped in a boat. After two days in a sea, they were rescued by a French ship, and were taken to Singapore. Then his brother's family spent three months there before they were permitted to enter the United States. His brother has been living in Philadelphia since 1981, and opened a Vietnamese restaurant in Chinatown. He is the only relative of Mr. Tran who live in Philadelphia.

Mr. Tran lives along North Fifth Street. The neighborhood is ethnically mixed with many Southeast Asians, Blacks, Hispanics, and working-class Caucasians. He works at the School District as a bi-lingual counselor assistant now. He has two daughters and two sons. Mr. Tran is a Buddhist, but he does not have time to attend the temple located in 12th and Spring Garden Streets.

He has made several friends in the United States. Most of them are former military officers like Mr. Tran. They meet on weekends, talking and drinking. They established an association called "Vietnamese Former Political Prisoners." For some time, Mr. Tran was President of that association. He was very active in this organization but after he got a permanent job at School District and a part time job teaching at the Asian Community Development Center, he could not find time to spend in that organization any more.

Mr. Tran is now a permanent resident of the Untied States and intends to obtain an American citizenship. As a relative newcomer, his life is still very difficult. His objective now is to work, to save money and to buy a house. He and his wife are having hard time to help their children complete their education.

SUMMARY

From the biographical sketches of different Asians living in Philadelphia presented above, we can catch a glimpse of the difference in social position between them. The illustrations presented above are by no means exhaustive and are not completely representative of three Asian American groups I studied. However, they reveal the major intra-group variations among each community. These people from various sub-categories within each ethnic group are actors who conceptualize and mobilize ethnicity in a variety of ways. Chapter 6 will deal with how these different individuals capture ethnicity—how they view themselves, recognize each other, and negotiate with the mainstream society.

NOTES

1. The national census result is congruent with Philadelphia sample. According to 1980 Census, the percent of Asians living in central city for the Chinese, Vietnamese, and Korean are 62.4, 55.2, and 46.6 respectively (Barringer, Gardner and Levin 1993).
2. All the names of interviewers used in this dissertation are pseudonyms for confidentiality.

Part II The Dynamics of Identity

6
Capturing Ethnicity

Personal identity is shaped by the members of a group themselves as well as by the members of other groups who interact with them. Unlike the concept of race, which pertains to specific physical traits, the concept of ethnicity connotes cultural group membership. Questions arise as to how members of an ethnic group develop an integrated sense of self inclusive of their past and present cultural contexts. An individual's ethnic identity may vary according to the influence of other individuals and the social context. The way in which ethnicity is experienced and expressed may vary among social groups according to their positions in a prevailing structure of power relations (Comaroff 1987). Power relationships among the various players in ethnic communities can affect the process of the negotiation of identity.

Self is a dynamic, multidimensional, and multifaceted structure composed of numerous self-conceptions. According to Triandis (1989), the self is considered to have three distinct dimensions: private (what I think of myself), public (what other people think of me), and collective (what specific groups of people think of me). During the process of ethnic identification, individuals select and incorporate information from their private, public, and collective selves.

Ethnic groups seek to explain or justify their choices through differing interpretations of the symbols. Because symbols are viewed as defining a shared view, members of ethnic groups seek to persuade one another of their respective views, whether as individuals or as members of associations or factions. An ethnic community is more than the aggregate of the choices of individual actors. Its orientations, cohesion, and structure are "a reflection of a constant push and pull between the different views and stances of the members in the course of their manipulation of shared symbols" (Cohen 1985). In addition, ethnic rhetoric, symbols, and rituals have to be revised to meet the test of acceptability imposed by the dominant group.

Many people I interviewed mentioned the fear of losing their own ethnic identity. For example, first generation immigrants are worried about their children losing their own ethnic heritage. But most of the time, Asian Americans could not articulate what the genuine elements of their ethnicities are. The interpretation of ethnic identity varies among members of the ethnic group. Conflicts of representation of ethnicity have existed among many community organizations. In order to create legitimate representation, many conflicting parties are involved. What then is the real, authentic Chinese, Korean, Vietnamese, or just Asian American ethnicity? Is it an entity or simply a construction? How do different ethnic members conceptualize their identity? We will look at how Asians view themselves and each other, and how different members of subgroups within ethnic communities conceptualize and interpret their identity in numerous ways.

PERCEPTIONS OF ETHNICITY AMONG ASIANS

Asian identity and Asian American identity are different because of the different socioeconomic contexts in which they are defined and expressed. Most immigrant generations of the Chinese, Korean, and Vietnamese Americans experience a sharp identity crisis because they suddenly become a racial and ethnic minority in America. The Chinese, for example, have imagined themselves at the center of the world (中國) throughout history. Historical documents show that the Chinese people have long categorized all non-Han (漢) minorities in China and white people from Western countries as barbarians. But when the

Chinese began to immigrate to the United States in 1850, they came under another form of racism, this time directed against them. The Chinese had lost their power to define others, and instead became the defined, the circumscribed. They soon became powerless in the American racial structure.

Most of my interviewees, without exception, responded that they can distinguish other Asian groups by physical appearance. From the physical apperance, behaviors, and gestures, they can even tell Chinese people from different parts of China. Although they cannot exactly describe how they distinguish these people, most Asians do carry around mental images of what other ethnic groups should look like.

In many cases, my respondents did not have a clear notion of their pan-Asian ethnic identity. Asianness is discovered after they arrive in the United States, partly because they are treated as one group by government and the general public alike. Each country has different histories of ethnic contact, and the Chinese, Koreans, and Vietnamese bring stereotypes of each other with them. Even though they are viewed as Asian Americans by outsiders, they clearly reinforce their ethnic identity based on their own culture. Some negative stereotypes raised by other Asian American groups against the Chinese are that they are selfish and untrustworthy, the Koreans are divisive and male chauvinistic, and the Vietnamese are rough and too individualistic.

Among many 1.5 or second generation Asian Americans, the discovery of ethnic identity begins after adolescence. According to my interviews, the use of ethnic language as well as interests in ethnic culture declines with age from preschool and elementary level to high school level, after which it increases somewhat at the college level. Many second generation Asian students confessed they suddenly "discover" ethnicity in college. At this level, they come to realize that they are always perceived as different in America and begin to associate more with the coethnics (or other Asian Americans) and regain their ethnic language ability (Chen 1992). Sun Yim, a high school teacher at Central High School in Philadelphia describes these phenomena in the case of Korean American students.

> Many Korean youngsters are not active in organizing Korean student associations when they enter high school. They mostly socialize with American students. Based on my observations at the Central High

School [in Philadelphia], most [Korean] kids suddenly become
interested in other Korean students in the 11th grade. You see a lot of
Korean kids active in Korean student associations in their last year in
high school, and there are more interactions between American born
Korean students and the students who recently arrived. (Interview
#47)

This Korean American students' case indicates that external forces
influenced their ethnic identification more than internal ones. To them,
the specific social context and the presence or absence of other Asians
were strong influences on their developmental process.

Many of my interviewees described values and beliefs that are very
general to many immigrant groups, for example, high values on
education and family are specific to their own ethnic group. In other
words, much of what is seen as distinctively Chinese is actually
common to Koreans and Vietnamese as well. Considering that these
three countries have been under a strong Confucian tradition, it is not
surprising that they share many cultural values and customs.

Chinese Americans

What is meant by Chinese and Chinese American? What are the
characteristics that describe Chinese American? The rich Chinese
culture, numerous cultural practices and rituals overwhelm even the
Chinese people. "It is so rich," Jennifer, a first generation immigrant
from Taiwan tells me, "that in order to understand the meanings of all
those symbols, you have to learn it [the Chinese culture]." Whatever
region the Chinese originated from, the Chinese strongly identify with
Chinese culture. In describing Chinese culture, most interviewees
centered on such values as strong familism, filial piety, and the
importance of education. Joseph, a second generation Chinese
American, described the definition of Chinese Americans in this way.

Code of ethics, filial piety, Confucianism, those aspects, the sense of
being an individual, freedom, self-reliance, I guess these are the
qualities that define Chinese Americans. The Chinese American
characters have been changing. Four or five years ago, I always
thought of Chinese Americans (this is the old perception, of course)
as people who are born Chinese or racially Chinese, but have

philosophically become Westernized. Right now, I could see that being a Chinese American doesn't mean rejecting Chinese culture, but taking the best part of both cultures. That's what I am trying to do. Part of me is trying to find the balance, looking at both cultures and trying to pick up the best of both cultures and to apply that to my world view. The worst quality is having to realize which qualities truly define you whether or not you should be American. You have to try to find the best. (Interview #48)

As a first-generation Chinese from Vietnam, Yen Le emphasizes the importance of the family in Chinese American experience, too. She identifies herself as Chinese even though she had spent most of her childhood in Vietnam. Like Yen Le, many Chinese from Vietnam work hard to connect themselves with Chinatown and Chinese community organizations.

Chinese Vietnamese, they take families first. Everything is done for families. It's quite opposite to Americans. That's because we are very close to family. We very care about family. If something happens to one member of the family, then I feel like as if it happened to me. Grandparents care about children, and children take care of parents. That is the big difference from Americans. (Interview #45)

Most 1.5 and the second generation Chinese I interviewed seemed to have a pride in visible physical symbols like Chinatown. The most prominent of these symbols is the Chinatown Gateway which was established in the early 1980s. It was a result of collaboration between Philadelphia Chinatown and Mainland China. The establishment of the Chinatown Gateway was intended to enhance the expressive attachment of Chinese culture as well as to promote tourism and commerce in Chinatown (Butcher 1990). Lei Lu, who owns a Chinese newspaper in Philadelphia expresses the importance of Chinatown on Chinese American identity.

Chinatown is most important. Philadelphia's Chinatown was established more than 110 years ago. It has a long story to tell. Some people are third generation or fourth generation of the original immigrants. On Race Street, there is a Hong Kong Chinese restaurant that was opened 50 years ago. Another grocery store on the Spring and 10th, was opened 80 years ago. They are still displaying old pictures. You see, the owners wear clothes of the Ching Dynasty! It's very exciting to go there and see those pictures. The original owner has passed away, and now his granddaughter and her son own the restaurant. So, the Chinatown is most important because Chinese tend to maintain identity very seriously. For the second generation it is hard because they are half American and half Chinese. When they come to Chinatown, they feel, "This is our root." (Interview #41)

In other words, Chinatown brings them a sense of home. Andrea Shih, a Taiwanese architect, agrees on the point that Chinatown provides a sense of community not only to residents but also to many Chinese who live outside of Chinatown. She has lived in Philadelphia's suburbs for more than 20 years, and has worked for many American companies. Now she owns her own architectural firm in Chinatown.

I have lived in my neighborhood for 20 years, but I don't feel I belong there. Even though our family are all very friendly to our neighbors, I don't really relate to them. We don't feel close to each other. I don't know if it's a part of American culture, I am not so sure. But when I became involved in Chinatown and the Chinese community, and when I moved my office here, I felt I had a sense of the community which I just couldn't get in my neighborhood. It's not so much as I feel more comfortable with Chinese, but eventually I feel that this is the place at least I belong to. When I walk up the street, people would say hello, because they know me, they chat with me. But when I walk on my street, besides my immediate neighbors, I don't get that kind of closeness. (Interview #87)

Father John is a Caucasian priest in the Holy Redeemer Catholic Church in Chinatown. He has become an important figure in Philadelphia Chinatown. Father John compares his service between the Black and the Chinese American communities. To him, the maintenance of the community based on the strong family ties is the most distinguishing aspect of the Chinese community.

I think that probably the most glaring thing that counts first is the difference in families of the people. The family seems to be stronger in the Chinese community than in the African or Caucasian community. Even though I haven't worked so much in White churches, I am pretty familiar with that . . . There is a strong sense of the community [in Chinatown]. If we have an event, we manage to build up it up to the point that it is an event for all members of the community. Everyone comes. No one wants to not be there if something important happens. There is a strong sense of wanting to be part of a group, part of a community. Children spend very little time with their parents, which strikes me as very interesting. Parents work very hard, and they pass on values to the kids without spending a lot of time with the kids. These kids have a lot of freedom, and very much have a peer group of kids that almost raise one another. They have a sort of superego. They definitely want to please their parents, and want to make their parents proud. However, the whole community all reinforces the same values. There are several churches in Chinatown, and many adults who work in the churches are voluntary. Neighbors, church, school, the other churches, they are all giving the kids the same message. So if some things are not right, kids know it. That helps kids to know when they get different messages, they think that something is wrong. That's not true for Black and White children in our country. They get so many conflicting messages from adults, and they don't want to trust anyone. (Interview #81)

The superego that Father John mentions is present in this 1.5 generation Chinese American's view.

Over the years, I have been more relaxed about filial piety. But every time I am relaxed, I start looking at what I am doing and how disrespectful with my parents then I realize how that's wrong. In that sense, I really try to tackle to my Chineseness. "This is wrong. You should try to change it." Knowing that your parents have gone through so much for you, this is wrong. That's why I feel it's more important to be Chinese than American. Of course, I am not saying all Americans are disrespectful to parents, but that is part of my perception of what being American means, it also equals being disrespectful. [Being American means] More individually centered, I guess. Being Chinese means putting others above you. (Interview #48)

Quite contrary to this rosy picture Father John provided, however, many Chinese American children take on the burden of learning to care for themselves from a very early age. Parents are away much of the time, and therefore provide limited guidance to their children, and many Chinese American families suffer a loss of effectiveness. While the community makes many attempts to pass traditional culture on to the children, I wonder if the adolescents grasp the significance and the procedures of these traditional holidays or festivals. As one of my 1.5 generation Chinese Vietnamese tells me, "It is good to keep traditions alive, but to tell you the truth, I really don't care about the fundamental meanings behind them" (Interview # 59).

In addition, the feeling of this closeness itself does not occur automatically to everyone in the community. Jennifer, a Taiwanese who speaks Mandarin, immigrated to the United States in 1992, and married a Jewish American. While living in Center City, she seldom goes to Chinatown. She does not feel quite at home in Chinatown.

> Somehow, I don't feel close to Chinatown because most of the residents in Chinatown are from Hong Kong. They speak Cantonese, and that's not our language. I don't feel that Chinatown is Chinese town. In fact, the Chinese are composed of three different countries, and the behavior and language are different. (Interview #82)

Chinese Americans in Philadelphia include speakers of many different Chinese dialects. Mandarin and Cantonese dialects are the two dialects with the greatest numbers of speakers. While the status of Cantonese in the United States has been established by the early immigrants since the last century, Mandarin has surpassed the standing of Cantonese in the United States and is regarded as the identity marker of Chinese today (Chen 1992).

Because the Cantonese-and Chaochou-speaking Chinese depend on the Chinatown economy in Philadelphia, most of them live in and around Center City where it is easier to find work, public transportation, and housing. However, the majority of Mandarin-dominant speakers, particularly from Taiwan, can afford to live in suburban areas where they think there are better neighborhoods and schools for their children. Socioeconomically, those who speak Cantonese and Chaochou are usually of the working class and have mostly immigrated from Southeast Asia or Mainland China, while most of those who are Mandarin speakers are from Taiwan and are professionals or small business owners. These residential differences contribute to the fact that Mandarin-dominant speakers make few attempts to make contact with Cantonese and Chaochou speakers and to learn the Cantonese dialect (Chen 1992). Instead, business owners in Chinatown begin to learn Mandarin to serve a multidialectical population.

From my interviews I also found negative evaluations about being Chinese. While many Korean and Vietnamese interviewees respect the Chinese for their good business skills, they sometimes mentioned that the Chinese are greedy and untrustworthy. Many Chinese hold the view that as a national ethnic group they are divided, and believe that particularly Koreans are united. Li-chiu, a 1.5 generation office worker who immigrated from Hong Kong, describes it in this way.

Ethnographer (me): What would be the worst characteristics about Chinese Americans?

Li-chiu: I think the worst thing about Chinese people is that they cheat a lot. I can't stand when I see that. The time that I feel I least wanted to be a Chinese is when I see people cheat. Unlike Koreans, we Chinese do not always help each other.

E: Well, neither do Koreans.

L-C: Really? I always thought that Koreans are united, and the Chinese are divided along different interests.

E: Is that so? I hear just the opposite assessment from Koreans.

Korean Americans

Korean immigrants, upon arrival in America, suddenly discover themselves as part of a minority. Their history of ethnic contact has been limited. It is only after they have been abroad that they see themselves in an objective way. By seeing one's society from the outside with the eyes of "the other," Koreans find themselves experiencing a marginality and strangeness. Mr. Byon, who works as a cashier in a Korean-run discount store in North Philadelphia, tells about the discrepancy between his life here and the expectation of it before his arrival in the United States.

> Our life here is quite different from what I thought it would be. We are primarily living with Blacks, and do businesses with them. It's very hard to live here. Of course, I am better off now than I was in Korea. But I really don't enjoy my job. I seldom have my own free time. I don't like the idea of working in a Black neighborhood for the rest of my life. It is not what I thought to be the American way of life. (Interview #15)

Korean Americans exploit resources on a mostly organizational level, partly because of their lack of a residential core. Their identity is largely maintained by these diverse social networks and personal networks, usually sponsored by local churches. Other Asian groups view this organizational proficiency as the main source of success among Korean American businessmen, as illustrated in a conversation with Li-chiu (see previous section). For example, Vietnamese had some previous contacts with Koreans. Those who had seen Koreans during the Vietnam War remember how tough and well disciplined Korean soldiers were. Since most of my Vietnamese respondents came from South Vietnam, they did not show any hostility toward Koreans who fought on their side. Vietnamese businessmen seem to respect Koreans as being so hard working and entrepreneurial. This is also true for Chinese Americans. Andrea Shih observes the diversity of Korean businesses in comparison with the Chinese Americans.

> I have a great respect for Koreans. If I compare Koreans with Chinese, I think the Korean people work much harder than the Chinese. They are willing to go to unsafe neighborhoods, and they work long hours, and they stick to those neighborhoods. I don't think a lot of Chinese people are working as hard as Koreans and are willing to get into those neighborhoods. Another difference is the diversity of businesses they own. It seems most Chinese are involved in restaurants, food related businesses. The Koreans have more diversity in business. (Interview #87)

However, this organizational proliferation among Korean Americans reveals the division and rivalry among the members of the community, as we will see in detail in the next chapter.

When I asked Chinese interviewees what they think about Korean people, many of them mentioned the extreme male dominance in Korean families. Even though the male dominancy is strong in many Asian countries, Koreans are regarded as the worst. David, a recent immigrant from Hong Kong responds to my question.

Ethnographer: Tell me what you think about Koreans.
David: I heard a lot of stories about Korean men. They never help wives, never wash dishes, always want to be served. Is that true? We Chinese are not like that.

Susan is a Jewish student who has been involved with the Korean community in Cherry Hill. She has made a lot of Korean American friends in her neighborhood, and occasionally baby-sits for a Korean American church. From early experience with many Koreans, she once thought about marrying a Korean man in high school. "All of my Korean American friends said no," she remembers, "Never a man who is a Korean national." Her Korean American girl friends would marry a Korean American, a boy who was born and raised here. They wanted the same kind of relationship that most American women want, an equal relationship, with domestic balance.

It always disturbs me: the relationship between parents and children, and the attitudes of Korean men—Korean national boys. If my friend cooked or we cooked, he always expected us to wash the dishes. Most of the men I know don't treat their wives the way American men do . . . One of my friends' parents were proud of their daughter, but they always wanted their sons to achieve. One of my friend's parents, even though they spent no money on their sons, since he is ROTC, will not spend money on their daughter. When my friend—a French major—asked her parents if she could go to Europe for summer, she was refused. They feel that a proper Korean Christian girl should not go. She wasn't allowed to do anything. She had no freedom. Social life was not important. The most important thing was getting good grades, getting into a good college, and going to church.

Now you look at the grades. A great young lady who has straight A's, but who did nothing. She never belonged to a club. Her mother still expected her to look after her little brothers, even though the older one was older than she had been when she started sitting for them. She had to go home every day at 3:00 PM. When she applied to college, the administrators already had a stereotype of Asian students; to them she was just another unimaginative Asian student. In my friend's case, she wanted to do other [extra-curricular] things, but her parents would not allow it. (Interview #13)

Obviously, this kind of negative stereotype bothers 1.5 or second generation Korean Americans. The characteristics which are believed to be Korean in origin are readily applied to the American-born Korean Americans as well. Robert Chun, an 1.5 generation Korean American remembers many of his Chinese American girl friends told him how their mothers warned them about dating Korean men because Koreans tend to be thoroughly chauvinistic. "That was the first time I ever heard something like that!!," Robert tells me, "I guess the Korean men those specific Chinese families encountered must have left a bad impression on them" (Interview #63).

Vietnamese Americans

Vietnamese customs have been enriched by adopting the distinct doctrines of Confucianism, Taoism from the North, Buddhism from the South, and Catholicism from the West. After 1,000 years of Chinese domination and 80 years under French colonialism the Vietnamese still have their own distinct customs. It is these customs and traditions that they believe should be preserved and passed on to the future generations. A first generation Vietnamese woman mentions the struggle of her people and the endurance of culture as important aspects of Vietnamese identity.

Vietnam as a country may be poor, but we as a people are very strong. We are a proud group of people. It is ingrained in our blood and culture. People throughout the centuries have either tried to eliminate or erase our culture but we always fought back and won. The Chinese tried, the French tried, the Americans tried, but they all failed in the end. Being in America and experiencing all I have is a part of the hardship that I chose to endure because I wanted to raise my children to be the best. Your children are all that you have. They are a reflection of you when you are gone. (Interview #66)

Nancy Ng is a college student who came to the United States at a very early age. Although she has little memory about Vietnam, she strongly identifies herself as Vietnamese.

I see myself as Vietnamese. I feel myself as a Vietnamese person. My mind, my heart and my blood have had their roots in Vietnamese traditions for centuries. Sometimes it is very hard to pinpoint one reason why I feel so strongly and am proud of my Vietnamese heritage. It could be because of my upbringing. My parents have always fostered in me the love and pride that they have for our motherland. It could be from our history. I know that my people have struggled to stay free and independent from outside invaders for centuries. We take pride in the fact that our culture, language, and ideology have not been erased from world history. Maybe, my identity of myself comes from the constant reminder experienced through racism and bigotry that I am different from the majority Caucasian population. Whatever the reasons may be I know that I am different and I am proud of those differences because I know that they make me strong and unique. (Interview #69)

As expressed by Nancy, the unique experience of the Vietnamese people is their endurance. Tai Nguyen, a 1.5 generation Vietnamese American college student also mentions this point.

Even though I have lived in the United States most of my life I still consider myself Vietnamese American because my parents have instilled in me a pride in my heritage. Though I don't think I will be able to live in Vietnam, I still think it is my duty to aid in the development and improvement and hopefully eventual freedom of my country in anyway that I can. I think that my successes so far can be attributed to the fact that I did not try to conform to the WASP ideal that I was surrounded with nor did I become alienated and isolated because of my different background. Instead my differences became a strength from which I could build a strong and healthy personal identity. (Interview #67)

The self-evaluation of Vietnamese Americans varies, but one common theme that most Vietnamese agree on is that they are sometimes too individualistic and do not cooperate with each other. "Because Vietnamese think they are the best, they don't work together much," one first generation Vietnamese American (Interview #57) tells me, "you can see a lot of distinguished Vietnamese, but you can hardly find distinguished Vietnamese organizations here." Dr. Tran, a first generation Vietnamese American educator at the School District of Philadelphia, explains the scarcity of Vietnamese community organizations in a historical context.

> Strangely enough, more Cambodian associations survive than Vietnamese associations. I think that Vietnamese people tend to be more alert, faster, and they are considered as underdogs. Usually Vietnamese people are paranoid about being used, so they don't bother what Americans advise them to do so. Cambodian people appear to have a more practical approach than just obey and follow the American ways to survive. Also, Vietnam was dominated by different countries by Chinese and French and America. Vietnamese intellectuals try to satisfy themselves by neglecting the majority people. (Interview #60)

In the Vietnamese American community, especially among welfare groups, the degree of solidarity is not maintained by positive cultural elements, but rather by their sense of shared experience and mistreatment from the mainstream. Residentially, they are rather "forced to" form a district. Voluntary organizations are not numerous compared to the Chinese and Koreans. Many of the organizations which serve the Vietnamese community are social work organizations such as the Southeast Asian Mutual Assistance Association (SEAMAAC), an umbrella association which binds together such Asian groups as the Vietnamese, Cambodian, Lao, and Chinese Overseas (Chinese Vietnamese) Association.

Many refugees have experienced devastating losses of relatives and friends, and have personally undergone terrifying ordeals as prisoners in reeducation camps and jails, or as "boat people" fleeing Vietnam; virtually all have experienced a sense of guilt at leaving behind loved ones in Vietnam whom they probably will never see again. In America, they find that many of the values and social arrangements that they cherish wither when confronted with the American leveling process.

When I asked other Asian groups about their perceptions of the Vietnamese, most of them were negative. Many Vietnamese youths are being scapegoated for increasing violence in Chinatown. It is fostered by both the mainstream media and residents in Chinatown. As a 1.5 generation Korean American reporter once told me, "Man, I almost got killed at one of the Vietnamese parties. I happened to be there. They [Vietnamese teenagers] started to tease me. They are really rough people. You better not touch them." Li-chiu, a 1.5 generation Chinese American also talks about how she perceives the Vietnamese differently from other Asian Americans.

> There's always a time there's a problem when it comes to the Vietnamese in Chinatown. Because these people have come from an area of war, they seem more violent to me. I can't say Chinese Vietnamese are not, I am sure there are some. But they are people who are different. Most Vietnamese people that I know are Catholics. They are very religious people. But I also see other groups of Vietnamese people who have problems or cause problems all the time. I cannot say why, but sometimes I think it's due to the war or the environment they had before. But I also see good sides of Vietnamese people. Everywhere there are good and bad. There has been a less problem now, you know, but when they first come here, we did have problems because of the group. I guess it's due to a lack of communication, language barriers. (Interview #46)

The Vietnamese were particularly upset by media reports that emphasized such topics as criminal gangs, which they considered wholly unrepresentative of the overwhelming majority of the Vietnamese American people.

Another popular perception about Vietnamese Americans shared by other Asians is that they live on welfare, "like Blacks" (Interview #88). Representing Vietnamese Americans as refugees means portraying them as passive recipients of that action. As DuBois (1993) notes, "the very model of the refugee discursively constructs a Southeast Asian who is incapacitated by grief and therefore in need of care. The model casts the Southeast Asian as *passive* and calls for the [social service] professional to assume an *active* role in caring, counseling, or intervening (emphasis DuBois's)." The horrible experience of Vietnamese refugees and their consequent flights to America represent all the good things about America.

ASIAN AMERICANS' VIEW OF AMERICAN SOCIETY

National surveys show that mainstream American society views Asian Americans quite negatively. It is interesting to look at how Asians view American society because it provides a critique of social relations and the racial landscape of American society. Asians arrive with numerous images and expectations of American society. Some groups such as the Korean American and Chinese American professionals are far better equipped than Vietnamese refugees. Nevertheless, their notion of America has been changed since their first arrival. Although many of my first generation Asian interviewees take the American dream at face value, they seem to realize that a minority member cannot fully become an "American" in this society. A first generation Korean American small business owner tells me how the expectations and images about America he previously held have changed dramatically.

> By coping with Americans, I found living as part of a minority to be very hard and unbearable. What I now experience is different from what I thought it would be. The streets are dirty, and doing business here is very dangerous. I sometimes wonder how a country like this has become so rich and powerful ... I once heard that early American settlers first built churches, then schools, and then their own houses. Now look at America today. Once a country of the disciplined, now suffers from drugs and violence. (Interview #16)

What is interesting about this person's remark is the assumption of American society as "white people's land," with beautiful landscapes and wonderful opportunities. This image is very much shaped by his exposure to the media and pictures from their own home country. Sometimes this image shatters, and sometimes it stays. Many immigrants contend that Americans do not know how to raise children in a good way and attribute the increase of crimes to the failure of family education.

When first and 1.5 generation Asian Americans say "Americans," they usually refer to whites, and I found they use specific terms when they mention Blacks, Hispanics, and other Asians. What, then, are some of the perceptions about white Americans held by Asian Americans? Generally, my respondents held favorable views about white Americans, as revealed by this 1.5 generation Chinese American.

> [White] Americans are very friendly, I mean they are very open people not like Asians. I think Asians tend not to speak as much or they speak to their own group. If you are on the street, Americans are always going to help you. I can't guarantee a Chinese would. If you are lost somewhere, there are always Americans who can help you. I think most Americans that I have interacted with always helped me. (Interview #46)

In cultural terms, Americans are regarded as being too individualistic and lenient about educating children. "Americans let their children do whatever they want," "Whether they jump up your car, or kick your door, they just watch them" (Interview #43). Sometimes Asian youngsters utilize this aspect to fool their parents. They try to get away with things by convincing their parents that American culture lets them do these things.

Contrary to what Waters (1990) found, Asian Americans can describe America as a culture, or in a more detailed way, some aspects of Western culture. They sometimes contrast the cultural differences in such general terms such as "East" versus "West." Conformity, respecting the elders, and harmony in the family are often used to distinguish Asian American families from American counterparts. The difference between mainstream American culture and the ethnic culture comes from the relationships, as illustrated by Joseph. Many second generation students confessed about how striking it was to be in a homeland.

The time when I feel truly American is when I go back to Taiwan.
When I am back in Taiwan, I truly know how different I am. That's
when I really see big part of my American side. But when I am in
America, I just see how different I am from Americans. So that's
when I see a big part of Chinese American side. (Interview #48)

There is a generational difference regarding perceptions of what
America should be. While the first generation Asian immigrants
naturally accept America as white-dominated, the American-born
generation stresses that America has always been a mixture of
immigrants and that the definition of Americanness has always been
reshaped. Shawn Chan is a third generation Chinese American who
grew up in the Philadelphia area. His grandfather emmigrated from
Hong Kong at the turn of the century. From his childhood, he
socialized with people from diverse ethnic backgrounds. Many Chinese
families he has had relationships with are from the upper-middle class.

I have a problem with the term "American." Because you just don't
know what the standard is. Is it German American's, is it white
Anglo Protestant American's? Do we hold that as a standard? What is
American? I believe what they call the "mosaic theory" which means
that every ethnic group holds its ethnicity and all the customs and
ideas come together, and become much more powerful. (Interview
#54)

One of the negative conceptions about White Americans is that
they are hypocritical, that "they seem to like you, but inside, you never
know what they are thinking" (Interview #59). Among my
interviewees, the Vietnamese group had the strongest disbelief towards
the systemic mistreatment by the white majority. Their mistrust against
outsiders was so strong that most of my Vietnamese American
interviewees were reluctant to be interviewed in the first place. It was
only after I revealed my identity as Korean that the tension somewhat
lessened. Yen Le, a Chinese Vietnamese social worker tells me about
her disgust at how Americans discriminate against people from
Vietnam.

I experienced many [much] personal discrimination here. When you work, if you have a better talent than them, they [other co-workers] tried to do something and let the boss kick you out. If you are not better than them, then they laugh at you. I know people work and save money to buy housing and cars, but American people don't realize that Vietnamese and Chinese Vietnamese work for 15 to 16 hours a day, seven days a week. And they say, "Oh! You just come to this country, and now you own a house and a car." They don't want us. They try to make someone into trouble. They try to break your window, break into your car, and make you move out to another place. That makes me sick. I plan to go back to my country when the situation becomes better. Many people say America is the number one country, but for me, it is just the opposite. They say America has freedom, but it's not. No freedom at all. How can you say we have freedom when you have five dollars in your pocket, and people try to take that five dollars from you? (Interview #45)

Universally, Asian groups have hostility toward Blacks, slightly less toward Hispanics, and mostly favorable opinions about other Asians. One first generation Korean interviewee, who did not clearly distinguish African Americans from Hispanic Americans, says, "those from the tropical land are all lazy, with lower IQs" (Interview #6). Obviously ignorance and stereotypes against other minorities do exist. Since Korean American store owners in African American neighborhoods spend most of their time at work they have very little contact with white America. Korean immigrants have a scant understanding of words like "prejudice" or "discrimination." Thus, it is understandable that the perception of America by Korean immigrants is incomplete (Chang 1992). A first generation Korean American woman self-criticizes the many Korean immigrants' attitudes toward African Americans.

Blacks are no different from Koreans. Both Blacks and Koreans have a history of oppression from the Whites and the Japanese respectively. There are many Blacks that are criminals and rob Korean-owned stores but also many Koreans are racist against Blacks. When I was in Korea, many movies depicted the Blacks as bad people. In almost every instance Blacks were perceived as criminals . . . We must never forget the Black involvement in the Korean War. Many Blacks went halfway around the world and risked their lives to free the Koreans from the threat of Communism. I could not imagine the homesickness the Black soldiers must have had when fighting to save Korea even though their mother country, the United States, did not give them a fair chance to live a normal life back at home. (Interview #65)

A similar, and a popular criticism compares the treatment of aliens in their homeland. Mr. Thai, a first generation Vietnamese who owns a small coffee shop in Southwest Philadelphia tells me it is natural for the majority to discriminate against the newcomers.

I did witness some racism or discrimination cases, but not many. If you live in your country, you still have discrimination toward foreigners. Maybe minority living in America is easier than those in Asia. I think if Americans live in Asia, they have to suffer more than we do right how. I am sure of that. Sometimes we feel uncomfortable and angry with discriminations, but think about how the Vietnamese would treat foreigners. (Interview #57)

Hearing voices from Asian Americans, we can realize that most of them are very sensitive to the relationship with outsiders, especially with the majority. History shows that the minority has defended the ideals of the mainstream society while facing constant discriminations. Being a minority means recognizing the difference and appreciating the importance of it. Father John provides an interesting observation concerning the relationship between Chinese Americans and the mainstream society.

I get calls frequently enough from people who have to do something in the broader community. They want to know how they should behave. Just the other day, a young man about 24 or 25 years old called me. He was born in the United States, and grew up in the Chinese school and the Chinese community. He's going to marry a Chinese woman next year. He speaks Cantonese although not very well. He told me that he had to go to the funeral for a Caucasian person, he wants to know what he is supposed to do whatever

happens to him [at the funeral]. "Explain to me what will happen. I
don't want to go there and be embarrassed." I explained different
things he should or should not do, and he was grateful. One young
man called me that his family was going to a wedding for someone
who is marrying a Caucasian. The interesting thing is when some of
our young people have to do something in a Caucasian community,
they call me sort of as an advisor. Never do Caucasians call me to ask
what he is going to do in the Chinese community. I think Caucasians
have a certain assumption that if they don't know what to do, they
[Chinese] will probably understand. They are not worried about being
embarrassed. They think if they go to a minority culture, the minority
culture would understand why they don't know what to do.
(Interview #81)

This statement by Father John tells us many important things about
race relations in the United States. The majority assumption has always
been, "Why can't *they* (the ethnic minority) be like *us* (the
mainstream)? The values of the majority becomes an unstated norm for
comparisons, not just an impartial reference point. Rather than making
a bold step to "be like them," to embrace different concerns, the
majority has been insensitive about the difference, as in the absence of
desire for advice among Caucasians in Father John's interview. On the
other hand, minority viewpoints can enlarge the understanding of
American society. As Okihiro (1994) argues, margins in American
society have provided a clearer perspective on the mainstream, its
assumptions, ambiguities, and contradictions.

REPRESENTING IDENTITY

Asians not only recognize differences between themselves, but they
seem to have incorporated the very notion of heterogeneity into their
image of being Asian. It is in terms of this category of difference that
Asians refer to and shape their concepts of the implications of being
Asian, their projections of how the community should be run and
developed. They justify their consequent efforts to impress these views
on their ethnic cohorts. Asian Americanness is not a natural excretion
of a genealogical tree, but a continual struggle among multiple modes

through a negotiation of the inescapable tension between secure definitions and a consciousness of the oppression that such definitions rest upon. The struggle in the shifting grounds of immigrant experience holds numerous possibilities for liberation and for the invention of new social arrangements.

Generation

Within the history of every immigrant group, a critical moment arrives when the second generation comes of age and challenges foreign born parents for positions of leadership within the ethnic community. The first generation painstakingly created and maintained such cultural characteristics as language, gender roles, and deference patterns. Now they are questioned and challenged by the American-born generation. Language change in publications, sermons, and business meetings is a key indicator of this transition. While the second generation often displays a strong commitment to the maintenance of ethnic organizations and institutions, an analysis of their ideological and programmatic character reveals significant innovations and adaptations reflective of a growing American-born membership and leadership.

In Philadelphia, the generation gap among Asian Americans has steadily increased. It is most apparent among Chinese Americans, and to a lesser degree among Koreans and the Vietnamese. The division between people "fresh from Asia" and the American-born population (often derogatorily termed "banana") exists. The older generation questions its value in the immigrant life, and young people desperately seek identity in subcultures. In the process, both generations miss important contributions of their culture that could actually strengthen them and make their adjustment more productive.

Regina is a Korean college student who recently came to the United States. She talks about how she was first upset to see the American born Korean Americans. To her, Koreanness comes from speaking the Korean language and maintaining the ethnic culture.

> When I first arrived in the United States, I felt disparate from the Korean Americans that I met. I did not want to be associated with them. They seemed, I thought, to have lost the culture and traditions that I have identified with all my life. I have branded them as people who were trying to fit into the system of the host culture by imitating

every move or action Americans made. I tried to banish these ideas later on, but they seemed to be permanently engraved on my mind. Why can't they adopt the American culture while simultaneously retaining their Korean ways? (Interview #64)

While this is not always the case, this sort of comment shows how Koreans back home, or at least first generation Koreans, view American-born Koreans. In Chinese, there are similar terms for describing the conflicting generations. *Jook Sing*, or the hollow part of the bamboo pole, is a derogatory term for the American-born Chinese meaning rootless and lacking in knowledge of Chinese traditions and culture. However, *Jook Kak*, (bamboo joint), meaning hard and unyielding, is used by American-born generation to degrade the Chinese-born counterpart for being too Chinese (Kendis and Kendis 1976).

Although a great degree of social mobility and intermarriage has occurred among Asian Americans in Philadelphia, there is a continuing supply of new immigrants who take the place of the older generations in the ethnic neighborhoods and occupations in Chinatown. The existence of a strong first-generation ethnic community, as well as of continued discrimination in housing and employment against racial groups, imposed constraints on many Asian Americans. Father John observes the relationship between the younger generation Chinese Americans and the newer immigrant generation in Chinatown.

The real early immigrants, those old families who had been in Chinatown for a long time, don't relate very well to the newer immigrants. It is partly due to the generation gap. They were here for a long time, and they were Americanized. Some of the Chinese people are embarrassed because here they have become very Americanized, and then these all new people come in. One young man said to me that he would never want to take his Black and White friends to Chinatown, to have them see these people. He would be embarrassed because they would think he was like them. (Interview #81)

Many of my interviewees recited the reality of a double-life, the ethnic private life and the "American" public life, with very little mediation between the two. In addition, communication between the two generations has not fully occurred. The American-born generation does not comprehend fully the old cultures and their values. Being raised in America just like other Americans and using the same institutions as other native born Americans, the meaning of Asian American for them is different from that of their parents. As a matter of fact, the first generation Asians can understand the situation in an abstract way, but they had not gone through similar experiences during their childhood. In short, the two generations have different starting points and different givens, as illustrated by this 1.5 generation Vietnamese American youth. The following segment is excerpted from a local Vietnamese American Catholic church publication.

> "Being Vietnamese" is more different for me than for my parents, or for my Vietnamese friends. History, traditions, music, all those things mean something special to them, maybe because it brings back memories of Vietnam, or friends and relatives from Vietnam whom they miss. I am not insensitive to their feelings, but try as I do, I don't feel their nostalgia in my guts. When I think about being Vietnamese, I think about my parents and my Vietnamese friends. I think about an "Anh" who tutored the Vietnamese language to me. It isn't because he tutored the Vietnamese language to me that I think of him as Vietnamese, but because he took time out to help me. And thus, I associate 'being Vietnamese' with people helping each other out and caring for one another. If being Vietnamese meant only sharing in nostalgia of people who self-righteously claimed to be 'more Vietnamese' than I am, I would have resigned from being Vietnamese before I knew what it meant to me.

As above statement shows, to many younger generation Asian Americans "being what Asian Americans are" is experienced on a gut level. In other words, Asian Americanness is not "a character" which exists out there, but "an experience" which can only be described in relation to other groups in a broader context. Asian American identity derives from a common experience of being yellow in a world defined by whiteness.

Asian Americans gradually acknowledged a distinct Asian American identity that had evolved over the years, based on the experiences of Asians in American. It was in the crucible of "Asian America" that their individual and group identities were shaped and had integrity. But before they could define "Asian Americanness," Asian Americans had to refute societal stereotypes that had degraded them. For Asian Americans, like other racial minority groups in the United States, capturing ethnicity is not a matter of individual, symbolic choice. They resolved their "identity crisis" by directly challenging the distorted images that have diminished them as individuals and degraded them as a group, replacing them with more accurate ones based on historical knowledge about themselves, and creating a pan-Asian counterculture that reflects their values and experiences (Wei 1993).

The second generation Asian Americans encounter problems in self-definition both from the ethnic community itself which insists on seeing them as "Asian," and from the mainstream culture, which also defines Asian Americans as Asians, or simply as being "the Other." The second generation's efforts to find out the voices of what it means to be Asian American has lead to the radical question of the meaning of Asian Americanness itself, and they try to find out alternative explanatory mechanisms for their own identity. As Chang (1988) and Park (1990) note, the emerging second generation now challenges the political structure of the Asian American community. For example, when students in Korea began to question America's role in the oppressive Korean regime and ordinary Koreans began to incorporate students' critical voices in the 1980s, the second generation Korean Americans criticized the Korean Association's attitudes toward democratization of the homeland and existing links between Korean American community leaders and the Korean government. Ethnic mobilization by the second generation may represent, as Bentley (1987) notes, "an attempt to revitalize existing self-conceptions and modes of domination, or it may reflect a particular kind of epistemological break, a shift in conceptions of personal identity as new modes of domination are instituted in response to changed environmental circumstances."

Class

One of the most significant factors in determining ethnic experiential variation is the variable of "class." Affiliation by class is not only known to cross-cut ethnic groups, but is itself an important source of variation within the ethnic group. The most common places of encounter of different ethnic and immigrant groups are the labor market and workplace. Often they confront each other as competitors. Identities are negotiated through interactions with these "others," both as models of ethnic performance to be emulated or spurned, or as sources of cultural elements to be assimilated or reflected. The internal dynamics, resources, and histories of the group are in themselves of major consequence in the process of ethnicization. Leadership, degree of institutional completeness, cultural particularity, and the power of the idea of peoplehood, all played a role. Young Min, a second generation Korean American college student, tells me.

> People say that you have a bond with people from your ethnic background, which is generally true. But the bond also comes from how people are brought up. There are some Korean people whom I won't be close with because they come from such a different background. Their fathers are doctors, and that's not the way I was brought up. In a sense, it is a totally a different background, the way they view life is so different. So my good friends are from similar a background who think the same way, many of whom happens to come from some Koreans. (Interview #37)

Frequently class and occupational background determine immigrants' view on racist America and the discrimination based on the ethnicity. Professionals seem to be less discriminated against at the working place in comparison with working class, or at least, they think so. Mr. Park is a first generation Korean American engineer who also owns a laundromat in West Philadelphia. Asked if he encountered any discriminations, Mr. Park responds in this way:

> Once you get hired, the next depends on you. You have to work hard, and they will respect you. In a way, the policy of hiring minorities sometimes help. Even though I had no benefits from being a Korean, there is an advantageous way to be a minority. The only thing to remember is the language barrier. It really hinders promotion. (Interview #31)

Although some Asian Americans are very critical about American society, typically the discourse ends with such comment as "We are the persons who took the choice, and therefore however it is hard, it's our responsibility after all." Some internalize the values of the white middle class. Despite their superior educational background and experiences, when faced with subtle glass-ceilings, many immigrant Asian American professionals say instead, "Perhaps I need additional training."

On the other hand, another reaction in confronting the glass-ceilings by Asian Americans is to quit the corporate world and start up a small business. Asian immigrant professionals are increasingly aware of their unstable and unclear future outlooks. It is frequently reported that Korean American engineers and office managers who used to work at American companies quit their jobs and started their own small businesses in inner-city neighborhoods. In addition, many professionals, including doctors, also run a small store, usually managed by their spouses, to supplement their family income.

Small business owners take rather ambivalent positions when it comes to ethnic and racial relations. Contrary to most professionals, they came to the United States quite recently. Take an example of Korean Americans. The Korean American small business owners have been exposed to the American media in Korea through movies, TV or radio programs stationed in Seoul. In many ways, these recent immigrants are ingrained with the stereotypes of minorities and the blatant racism portrayed by the American media. I discovered profound misunderstanding and misconceptions among Korean store owners about Blacks and Hispanics. In addition to this, the Korean Americans do not regard the small business as a symbol of a success but rather as temporary—and the only available—way to survive (Chang 1991). Often the ethnic tensions between Korean store owners and Black residents come from this different interpretation of a small business. The working class shares commonalities with other minority workers. They are very critical of other Koreans—mostly professionals and affluent businessmen—of being arrogant and racist.

Middle class immigrants experience a loss of power. They were the majority in their own countries, but now discover themselves in a position defined by difference. The immigrant middle class's desire to overcome this condition manifests itself through a grasping for familiar essentials to regain the power to remain unnamed. They are the ones who try hard to define "the Asian heritage and culture," and to promote the economic advancement on the American capitalistic model, simultaneously preserving an Asian essence. Immigrant Korean constructions of national identity are revealed to be predictably similar to dominant nationalist thought in Korea.

The changing composition of the Asian immigrant community is radically altering the contours of a community that was until recently predominantly composed of middle class professionals. The professionals see the illegal immigrant, the unpaid worker, and the ill-paid laborer in the United States as mere aberrations from the community's coveted place as a model minority. The Asian immigrant community tends to deny the existence of gays, lesbians, battered women, and illegitimate children as inconsistent with that Asian heritage under which it has taken refuge.

Gender

The household is the most important arena of social life among many Asian Americans. Family members contribute a great deal to the household economy. Barred from entering the white collar job market, many families are forced to start family-run, blue collar businesses, such as dry cleaners and discount stores, where the husband and wife work side by side. For the first time the husband has his wife as a co-worker, which greatly influences their marital relationship in both a positive and negative way. This Korean American small business owner tells me about the increasing role of women in the immigrant household.

> When people come to the United States, both husbands and wives work together. In other words, the man's power in home has been diminished here. That is one of the changes here. Personally, I want to preserve in an old way. But it is very good for my wife, I guess. She will never go back to Korea again. (Interview #1)

Now, they are working together, and the justification for the male being the sole authority is quickly diminishing. For example, any Vietnamese husbands living in America suddenly find themselves experience cultural shock when their wives and children acculturate faster than they do to American society and show little respect and obedience. Therefore, these men are more likely to suffer from depression, emotional trauma and psychotic bewilderment (Lam 1993). Males are already frustrated by seeing their education and occupational skills under-utilized, and suffer status inconsistency. They are helpless, seeing their traditional authority over their wives and children eroded. As a result of this need to prove their authority, Asian men continue to expect their wives to perform their traditional activity as homemaker while also working equal hours with their husbands.

The Asian woman becomes frustrated that her husband perpetuates inequality in their domestic relationship when their working relationship has become more or less equal. For Asian women, the sexism prevalent in both Asian and American cultures has an immense effect on their lives. It appears that Asian women have to act as a buffer for cultural shock and frustration. They usually have to bear their husbands' frustration often expressed in acts of aggression. Although employment of the wives may have substantial impact on the family-kinship system of Asian immigrants in the United States, their employment has little impact on their traditional family roles at home. For example, from my data, the traditional authoritarian and male-dominant values still exist in the Korean American home. In spite of their full-time employment, most of the immigrant wives are expected to perform family tasks as traditionally expected. Under this condition, they bear a heavy burden of performing their family tasks—both household tasks and child care activities. Stephanie, a 1.5 generation college student is upset about the paternalism and sexism in her family.

> I used to feel angry at my father because when he comes home after work, he does not help my mother at all. He just sits back while my mother, who also works the same number of hours as my dad, rushes to make dinner for the family. Her chores never end, yet she does not complain. Furthermore, even my older brother has been influenced by this chauvinistic attitude toward women and orders me around the house. Of course when I was younger, I would do it because he might beat me up. But today, when I no longer feel intimidated, I begin to feel guilty if I don't do what I am supposed to do. My mother still calls me from work when I am home during break telling me to cook something for my brother and if I complain, she starts a series of

lecture about how I am never going to find a husband because I am too lazy to cook and clean. (Interview #61)

The Korean Woman's Association has been a catalyst for the advancement of women's position in the immigrant Korean community. Its participants have been mainly middle-class Korean American women responding to oppression in both their ethnic and mainstream societies. They have tried to challenge the notion of Korean Americans, the middle-class value of Korean womanhood. But instead, they have somehow remained to reinforced middle-class hegemony. The most neglected and least active Asian American women have been working-class women, most of whom are recent immigrants and refugees. One member of a Korean American social service organization remarks, "To me, the Korean Woman's Association is an organization which educates its members about the woman's rights and the movements through seminars. I don't think women who are really in need go there for help."

I participated in one Asian American seminar session in Philadelphia which was directed at service professionals who deal with minority populations. One Caucasian woman accused Asian men of abusing their wives and children, and one of the panelists, a Chinese American man, presented a cultural defense. He stated that abuse is practiced in many countries in Asia as a way to discipline the family, and it is thus generally accepted in Asian culture. He infuriated both Asians and Americans in the audience and ignited a heated discussion. Although it is understandable that domestic violence among recent Asian immigrants is the expression of depression and loss of power, it cannot be justified. However, I should point out what was missing in their dialogs on this issue. The traditionally close-knit Chinese community intervenes and offers support before the situation becomes fatal. Such instances are mediated through extended family members rather than resolved in court. Unfortunately, in many immigrant's cases, there are not many resources for emotional support through such a mechanism.

Forgotten Minority

In conjunction with gender issues, I would like to address another population that is often invisible in the Asian American community.

Apart from the complexity in terms of class, gender, and generation, there are numerous groups of people who have not been represented in official statistics and community activities. These people are tantamount to a multiple minority who are discriminated against according to race, gender, sexual orientation, marital status, or a combination of these. To illustrate some of these people, I have selected Korean war brides, Amerasians, and the Koreans adopted by American families.

Korean women who are married to non-Koreans are scapegoated as victims by the underground criminal business that promotes prostitution. The public perception of the Korean women catering to American soldiers around the base community have been negative since the outbreak of the Korean War in 1950. Several examples of name-calling, such as *Yanggongju* (Bride of the West) or *Yanggalbo* (Whore of the West), directed at them have been indiscriminately used to denigrate those Korean women who contact the American solders. Even today, one can still observe the tendency among some people who show their reservations and social distance from those Korean women who intermarried with the American soldiers. Even those intermarried Korean women with a higher educational backgrounds who are married to non-military spouses tend to become overconscious of the public perception of them. The following extract is taken from a local Korean newspaper. Often Korean women who married an American soldier, or "War Brides," attend Korean churches without their husbands, and socialize with each other.

> I am so happy that you [Korean church members] accepted me. I have always had a guilty feeling about marrying an American GI. I just thank all of you that my son can learn Christian love and mingle with other Korean kids. (from a Korean American newspaper)

It was very surprising that this woman accepts prejudices among Koreans, saying that she has felt guilty for marrying an outsider, and now thanks people for allowing her to become one of "them" in an immigrant church. She is somehow indicating that she has finally been "purified" by Christian love. I must point out that many of these Korean war brides are the victims of Korean male-domination, and some of them took great steps to challenge the dominant structure by marrying Americans. However, their stories are largely unheard by Korean Americans, and important women's issues are rarely addressed in the Korean American community.

The migratory experience can lead to more embracing identifications on the margin of the host society. Those who do not think of themselves as Koreans before migration become Koreans in the diaspora. Ms. Kim, one of my interviewees, who works at a bank as a financial analyst, is the offspring of an African American soldier and a Korean woman. She had a hard time in adjusting to Korean society because of the negative stereotypes against biracial children. Ms. Kim sometimes relates herself to the African American community. Whichever part she chooses to identify—Korean, American, or Black American, she places herself in a minority. She rediscovered Koreanness after arrival in the United States once she found out that she could get along with Koreans better than African Americans. She goes to a Korean Buddhist temple.

> Back in Korea, people mistook me as an American because of my shape. I was never accepted as an ordinary Korean. But after I came here, I act more like Koreans. I get support from Korean women at a temple I go to. I can relate to them more, and I want to show my Koreanness. I became a patriot. I go to the Korean market and buy everything there. Even bras and panties. (Interview #5)

Kathleen, another interviewee, came to the United States as a baby. She was adopted by an American family through the Holt International Children's Services, which is responsible for many Korean adopted children in the United States. She grew up in the Los Angeles area in a Dutch American family. She has never been involved with a Korean community. Rather, she was profoundly influenced by her Dutch upbringing. She can speak Dutch and displays some Dutch cultural items like wooden shoes at home. The realization of her Korean heritage came later.

> Just recently I became strongly aware of my roots. A couple of years ago, I was in a very serious relationship with a Caucasian man, and the relationship didn't work out. I strongly felt the loss from the break-up, and began to think about who I am, how I relate, how I find

my sense of belonging, where I belong, who I belong with. As part of that process, I did some psychological testing, and see how some of the testings came out. The person who scored the tests was from Australia, and had been exposed to a lot of Asians and Asian cultures. He said, "Your results are distinctly different from most Caucasian results I have ever seen." And I said, "How can it be? I grew up in the United States all my life, and I don't know anything about Korea!" He continued, "You can't deny five thousand years of genes. They are still in you, they are part of you." There have been a lot of debates of the nature vs. nurture thing, I am sure. I am not saying that I totally agreed with what he said. But that experience got me thinking, and I started to think that maybe there is something Korean in me. And I began to talk to doctors and nurses where I work as a pastor that I wanted to be exposed to the Korean people and culture. (Interview #56)

Kathleen's example demonstrates the characteristics of ethnicity that were discussed before. In a separate interview, she reflects on her childhood among her Dutch brothers and sisters, and remembers how they treated her as "a China doll." While she grew up as a "white," she always realizes that she is different from the majority. However, since she has not retained any individual or collective memory about Korea, she could not grasp her ethnic identity. Her contemplation of "something genetically Korean" shows the dynamic process of primordial sentiments that can trigger the longing for ethnic identity.

Ms. Kim and Kathleen are not visible in the Korean American community. There is a negative stereotype attached to Amerasians. Many people are ashamed of abandoned or illegitimate children because of the strict Confucian ideology. Apparently, the Korean Association in Philadelphia has not reached out to these populations.

Illustration: Korean American Student Conference

I would like to present the eighth annual Korean American Student Conference as an example to illustrate the representation of identity by different players in the Asian American community. As a member of the Board of Advisors of the Conference, I was able to observe and participate in a variety of events and organizing committees. I would like to emphasize the dialog and negotiation which occurred between student groups and community organizations rather than to show events in minute detail.

The Korean American Students Conference (KASCON) has been one of the most important meetings which the second generation Korean American college students organize to discuss pertinent issues about their identity and community. It was first organized in 1987 out of a concern for understanding and empowering the Korean community in the United States, and since then the annual conference has been held in different cities around the country. One of the prime objectives in organizing a conference like KASCON is to let second generation Korean American students explore community issues and problems. Most Korean American college students have just rediscovered the meaning of their ethnic identity, and they have been motivated to learn more about it. To second generation students as future leaders of the Korean community, a national conference like KASCON can provide participants with a valuable opportunity to meet and talk with community activists and to share a variety of concerns in their own community.

The 1994 conference was scheduled to be held in Philadelphia, after a group of students at the University of Pennsylvania won the bid at the previous conference held in San Francisco the year before. As was the case at the last few conferences, the organizers of KASCON VIII were students from different colleges around the conference sites, such as Bryn Mawr, Haverford, and the University of Pennsylvania. Student organizers were divided into several different committees including Fundraising, Speaker, Advertising, and Program and Entertainment. However, they encountered difficulties at an early stage. First of all, these students were inexperienced in planning, financing, and running the big events like KASCON. In addition, they did not have prior contact with the Philadelphia Korean American community. Most of them were from out of state and had not been actively involved in Korean American community affairs. They needed a parent organization to guide and oversee the whole process.

Dr. Hong, a medical professor at Thomas Jefferson University who served on the Board of Advisors for KASCON two years ago, was very enthusiastic about helping the student organizers. He is a first-generation Korean immigrant who came to the United States in the late 1940s. Being a refugee from North Korea, he has a big sympathy in the lives of dispersed Koreans overseas. As one of the respected and influential persons in the Philadelphia Korean American community, Dr. Hong set up the Board of Advisors for the 1994 KASCON. In selecting members of the Board, he considered "people who were knowledgeable about the community and dedicated to help students, not those who wanted to obtain personal prestige out of it" (personal conversation with Dr. Hong). In doing so, Dr. Hong rather avoided people from the Korean Association of Philadelphia (umbrella organization) and other Korean business organizations, who were eager to be included in the Board for political reasons. For example, the Board declined the active participation of the Asian Law Center, an organization set up by a local Korean church. Naturally, members of the Board were composed of professionals such as doctors and professionals with no affiliation to Korean associations. Of the 15 member Board only two were women. Later on, the Board grew larger with the inclusion of 1.5 generation professionals, notably members of the Korean American Professional Association (KAPA).

The matter of the introduction of KAPA and its members to the Board was a little bit controversial since it was one of the organizations in the community. KAPA was an organization run by young Korean professionals to help educate second generation Koreans and to serve as a resource bank for recruiting them to the mainstream professional fields. It has grown rapidly over the past few years and was gaining recognition in the community. For their part, events like KASCON could be a vehicle for boosting their status in the community. The Board, however, needed young members who could bridge the first-generation Korean community and the second-generation students organizers, and who could mediate between the mainstream and the Korean community. Thus, KAPA was able to join the Board of Advisors without much opposition among existing members.

Many Korean Americans in Philadelphia were not aware of the conference at the beginning. Local students attending such elite private colleges were very few, and students from community colleges and other local colleges had not participated in the event. To them, KASCON was seen as "an annual festival for Korean American students from the upper-middle class background."[1] Indeed, many student organizers are from well-to-do families, and have grown up in predominantly white suburban areas. Their knowledge of spoken

Korean was limited, and some of them had never been exposed to the Korean ethnic community before. Thus it became necessary to publicize the event in the community, emphasizing its importance, and asking for support. It was important to represent the conference as "our event," so that everyone in the community could benefit from it. In connection with KAPA and some other Board members, reporters from local Korean newspapers were brought in, and they started running stories about KASCON.

With the help of the Board of Advisors, students began contacting the key organizations in the Korean American community in Philadelphia. They gradually learned the way to deal with the Korean community—keeping a low profile, following Korean manners, and manifesting many Korean things in the conference. Different organizations they contacted had different agendas. To attract as many people as possible all documents, including press releases, letters and pamphlets, were prepared both in English and in Korean (members of the Advisory Board helped in translating into Korean). In this process, the participation by the women's association was minimal. It became apparent that organizations run by Korean women had not yet been incorporated into the influential circles and the decision-making process in the Korean American community. Through these efforts, portrayal by the local ethnic media has been much improved, and various newspapers and newsletters began urging readers to support the event. The organizing committee scheduled a major fundraising drive in the Korean community—a dance party for second-generation college students and a dinner banquet. Unlike the dance party, the fundraising dinner banquet had to be a primarily first-generation event. Senior members of the Board also tried funding from the Korean source, pleading for help so that "our Korean students far away will not forget their cultural roots."

To advertise the fundraising dinner banquet, a meeting between student organizers and the Board of Advisors was arranged. At the meeting, tickets were allocated to members of the Board to sell to fellow Koreans of the organization they belonged to. It was not surprising to find that these individuals belonged to many different organizations—religious, formal, or voluntary—and there were overlaps among members the Board. The keynote speaker for the banquet was a political science professor at the University of

Pennsylvania, who addressed issues concerning the nuclear standoff between North Korea and the United States, and its implication for the future of two Koreas. The speech was given in Korean and Korean entertainment followed.

The Advisory Board recognized early on that they could not dictate the process of organizing the event, nor would they impose any kind of rules or ways students should follow. The selection of topics and issues was up to the second generation students, and thus many subjects which were Korean in nature and were not necessarily relevant to Korean Americans were left out. The theme for KASCON VIII was "Agents of Change: Empowering Ourselves and Educating Others," emphasizing empowerment as a self-sustaining process and education as a means to achieving this end. Special attention was given to women's issues since "this has been long overdue in the Korean American community, and the status of being a double minority cries out for special observance in our male dominated power structure" (program statement).

On the first day of the conference, The mayor of Philadelphia and the Korean Consulate General from New York made opening speeches. Korean American keynote speakers addressed a variety of issues about what it means to be Korean American. One of them, a third-generation Korean American woman who is a prominent scholar on Asian American literature addressed women's issues in the Korean American community. Another keynote speaker, a first-generation Korean American medical doctor, stressed the pivotal role in the Korean independence movement played by an early Korean American (Philip Jaisohn) who had lived in Philadelphia. He tried to make points to portray Philip Jaisohn as a role model of Korean Americans. To many first-generation immigrants Philip Jaisohn represents a prototype of a patriot who never forgot his mother country. Student audiences recognized the historical importance of his efforts toward building Korea's independence; however, they might see him differently in building Korean America.

An interview after the conference which was included in the Korean Herald, the newsletter for the Korean American Association of the Greater Philadelphia, shows that there are significant differences in viewing or representing Korean American identity through the conference according to generational differences. The chief editor of the newspaper, a first generation Korean, asked if the conference could be run in Korean, or if there could be one session devoted to a Korean speaking contest. The interviewer viewed the conference as a medium for learning and maintaining traditional Korean culture, whereas the student organizers viewed it as a forum for understanding and discussing contemporary issues about Korean Americans. As a matter of fact, two thirds of the interview questions were related to the importance of the Korean language.

SUMMARY

The ethnicity perceived and manifested by individuals and groups clearly shows the situational and instrumental aspects of identity-making. Three Asian ethnic groups have become an ethnic and racial minority once they arrive in the United States. The Chinese, Koreans, and the Vietnamese already had stereotypes about each other. Regardless of their country of origin, Asian Americans gradually recognize a distinct identity based on their common experiences in the United States. Images about themselves and the host society changes over time. In the heterogeneous Asian American community generation, class, and gender all play an important role in shaping the kinds of ethnic identities taken by various subgroups, as is illustrated by the Korean American Students Conference case. The next chapter will continue discussion on the dynamics of ethnic identity, focusing on the force of continuation and change.

NOTES

1. This matter is yet to be resolved. Sessions concerning second generation were dominated by identity crisis and diversity in career goals. The variety of second-generation experiences in terms of class were not discussed fully, partly because of the lack of such student representation in the organizing committees.

7

Boundary Maintenance and Reproducing Culture

Elements of ethnicity are significant as symbols in the maintenance of boundaries. Through the maintenance of symbols, ethnic group members interact with each other. Language, tradition, and the festivals that immigrants participate in and celebrate, even though the contents of them may not be derived from the culture of origin, are nevertheless believed to be distinctively ethnic. Ethnic institutions are vehicles for representing identity and producing culture. A variety of institutional mechanisms are used by ethnic groups to stimulate internal interaction and communication, such as regional and interest organizations, religious organizations, ethnic newspapers and broadcasting stations. While intermarriage between groups of different race and ethnicity has occurred more frequently than before, still strong in-group marriages are practiced. In this chapter, I will look at how Chinese, Korean, and Vietnamese Americans use ethnic symbols differently, and how these symbols are utilized through a variety of institutions. It is my basic premise that these processes are changing over time since ethnic boundary maintenance is situational in nature.

ETHNIC LANGUAGE

Language is one of the cultural attributes that has the strongest effect in maintaining solidarity in an ethnic group. It is a fundamental source of ethnic identity since it is learned at a very early age, primarily within the context of the family. A nationwide survey indicates that more than 80 percent of the Chinese, Korean, and Vietnamese Americans speak a language other than English at home (Barringer, Gardner and Levin 1993). From my interviews and observations of Asian American families, it is clear that the majority of the parents intend to instill in their children the traditional values of filial piety and teach them the ethnic language. Local churches and organizations run ethnic language schools on Saturdays and Sundays so that children may attend both the public schools and the ethnic language schools. For most youngsters, ethnic languages are used at home, in more private occasions. Lei Lu, who owns a Chinese newspaper, gives some reasons for bilingual education.

> My kids have to know and speak fluent English. No question about that. They are Americans, they are going to live in the United States. But they have to know Chinese too. Even though they are born here, their neighbors will not treat them like other Americans. They treat them as Chinese even though they speak the same fluent English as other kids. If they can't speak Chinese, it would be bad for them. They've got to learn both. It's good for them. (Interview #41)

For many young Asian students, coping with school problems and homework from two kinds of school systems is a double burden. The majority of students who attend the ethnic language school do so under pressure from their parents. However, second generation students have very little interest in the language schools. Thus their interests gradually fade away.

To many of my second generation respondents, the ethnic language became a private language which was only used within the family. However, among 1.5 generation, the ethnic language can communicate important meanings that English cannot convey. For example, to hear 1.5 generation Korean Americans talking, you will notice the distinctive way of mixing Korean and English—putting English words in a Korean grammatical structure, or vice versa. It is frequently observed that the use of ethnic languages in certain mixed social contexts really serves to exclude outsiders and reinforce ties between insiders. Even though these 1.5 generation Asian Americans are capable of speaking English perfectly, they selectively use ethnic language.

Many of my second generation respondents discover their identity only after their college years. Actually a lot of children lose their language until they rediscover their identity in college. Sometimes the interest in acquiring ethnic language is coupled with practical reasons. "It is good to know Chinese," one of my Chinese American informants tells me, "you get discounts or good buys in Chinese stores, or even get quick service in restaurants." Many of my college student interviewees talk about the possible career options related to Asian countries and the importance of acquiring Asian languages in order to pursue their career in that direction. They try to recapture the ethnic language through courses in school. Asian Americans also begin to realize that the maintenance of culture through language and traditions is a form of resistance, a stand against cultural domination which threatens to destroy identities.

HOLIDAYS AND RITUALS

Rituals remain as signs of ethnic identity, when other traditions have faded, partly because of their ability to symbolize complicated meanings. An ethnic group recognizes and displays its own distinctiveness through such periodic celebrations. When a family or community gathers together for rituals, matters of ethnicity, religion, and other key features of identity become more obvious, as normally private values are proclaimed more publicly.

Anthropologists and folklorists have been interested in ethnic traditions and rituals, which are maintained, modified, and invented in new environments. The retention of cultural elements is important insofar as they lead to high rates of exclusive interaction and serve as symbols to maintain boundaries between groups. Life cycle rituals—birthdays, weddings, or funerals—are signs of continuity and change. Different ethnic communities in the United States revitalize holidays and life cycle events in different social contexts. A first-generation Korean American gift shop owner describes traditional Korean customs people practice in the Korean American community.

> Somehow, Korean Americans keep up traditions more than Koreans back home these days. They try to follow exactly the ways things are practiced in these events; weddings, birthday ceremonies, or whatever. Of course, they embraced a lot of American ways, but that doesn't mean they discarded old customs. In my view, they long for traditions. They take it very seriously, not to lose their culture. (Interview #6)

In describing Chinese American weddings, Father John notices some Chinese elements and their mixture with the traditional Catholic wedding ceremony. Generally speaking, the wedding ceremony itself is practiced in the American way, whereas banquets and big parties after wedding ceremonies are regarded by many people to be Chinese in character.

> What happens is, first of all, that we have to deal with the date of a wedding whether it is a lucky day or a unlucky day in a lucky year or not. Last year I had twelve weddings. But no weddings in 1994. In Cantonese tradition, the word for death and a word for 4 sounds similar, so that's one reason why some people told me they won't get married this year. A number of times, weddings change because of the dates. Also sometimes I found that kids don't believe [Chinese traditions], parents do. Caucasians who marry Chinese people had awful trouble with their own priests because they don't understand why Chinese families are insistent on a particular day. Catholic weddings are on Saturdays. But sometimes Chinese families prefer Sundays or Mondays. The wedding ceremony in church is a very traditional American wedding. I never find anybody asking to do anything except that. However, the banquet is somewhat traditionally Chinese. That's always very Chinese. Sometimes they have ceremonies before they come to church. The bride does change clothes a couple of times, but the bridegroom does not. They go from table to table pretty much how they do in Hong Kong, like making a toast at each table. There are many speeches beforehand

acknowledging all the relatives there. Those are Chinese kind of things. (Interview #81)

While many ethnic holidays have faded away, new holidays are attracting different meanings. In the Chinese community, by far the biggest and the most widely known celebration is the Chinese New Year. Fireworks, the dragon and lion dances, and the colorful banners are commonly seen. Next to the Chinese New Year the Mid-Autumn festival is most popular and is celebrated by many Chinese families on the fifteenth day of the eighth month of the Chinese calendar. At celebrations, moon cakes—large round cakes made of flour and brown sugar, filled with lotus or bean paste—are eaten. Unlike the Chinese New Year, for most of the Chinese families living in Chinatown, this festival is celebrated privately at home.

Koreans, on the other hand, were split over New Year's Day. Called *Sol*, the lunar New Year's Day is an important day for ancestor worship and for paying respects to one's elders. The more important issue here is whether the meaning stays the same or is somewhat modified. For example, *chusok* is sometimes replaced by Thanksgiving. *Chusok*, or the Korean Harvest Moon Festival (same day as the Chinese Mid-Autumn Festival), is a holiday equal in importance and significance to New Year's Day. It is also celebrated according to the lunar calendar, and is a family holiday for honoring one's ancestors and giving thanks for a bountiful harvest.

Now, I will to discuss the celebrations of life-cycle rituals and holidays in connection with maintaining identities and ethnic boundaries. To illustrate this, I selected two Korean rituals, one Vietnamese holiday, and another Chinese event that I attended.

Case 1: Korean American Wedding

In most cases, wedding ceremonies are conducted in a church in the American way, but it is customary to have a Korean style banquet after the ceremony. However, among some Korean American businessmen, wedding ceremonies are usually held in the evenings, since many Korean guests who own small shops normally work on weekends and cannot attend the ceremony during the day time or on weekdays. Some weddings are held in a big restaurant so that the guests can eat together after the wedding.

I would like to describe one of the Korean American weddings that I attended. It was a marriage between a Korean American bridegroom and a Korean bride who pursued a graduate degree in the United States. Families, relatives, and friends of the bride flew from Korea to attend the ceremony at a local Korean American church. The ceremony itself was conducted in the American way. After the wedding ceremony at the church, guests were invited to a banquet at a nearby country club. The reception was a mixture of American and Korean style. Food was served in a three-course American style. Speeches by the father of the bride were given in both English and Korean, and music and dance followed. Finally, the newly-weds changed their clothes to traditional costumes and offered *Pyebaek*, a Korean tradition of bowing to the bridegroom's parents and relatives, meaning a symbolic welcome of bride to her new family. Traditionally, *pyebaek* is not offered to the bride's parents and relatives, but the couple decided to offer it to them as well for an indication of domestic balance. However, at the last minute, the bridegroom's mother insisted on *pyebaek* for only the groom's relatives since time was running out. The bride's parents reluctantly conceded. While this whole process involved a bit of a struggle for prestige between the bride's and bridegroom's families, American guests were very amused at this traditional ritual. In Korean American weddings, *Pyebaek* was the only item that could display Korean ethnic identity during the wedding, thus it was conducted very seriously.

Case 2: The Korean 70th Birthday

Chilsoon, or the 70th birthday, was held in the garden of Mr. Lim. The immediate families and their relatives along with friends from a church gathered in this one of the most important events in a person's life. For a person to reach 70 has been a rare occasion in the past, so the event was called *Gohui.* It is an occasion for descendants to show their respect for parents.

The ceremony started by Mr. and Mrs. Lim's procession to the "honorees" table in front of the stage in the backyard of his daughter's house. Rarely is *Chilsoon* celebrated in a daughter's house since the celebration for parents' birthday is a responsibility for the eldest son. Since Mr. Lim lives with a daughter, who is better established than his son, the site for the party was decided to be Mr. Lim's daughter's house. A violin quartet, one of whose members is Mr. Lim's granddaughter, performed Mozart during the procession. Mr. and Mrs. Lim sat with a minister at the church they go to, who was invited as the guest of honor. Their sons and daughters made traditional bows on a mat set up in front of the table. Their grandchildren followed making bows. After each bow, family members offered Mr. Lim rice wine to show their respect and reaffirm their familial ties to the celebrant. They thanked their parents for taking care of them and thanked the community for coming to share this event with the family.

After the offering, the master of ceremony gave a biographic sketch of Mr. Lim and his life achievements. The minister followed him addressing the meaning of growing old and spoke of the importance of family unity and solidarity in keeping the elderly connected in their social interactions. The sermon emphasized cultural differences in the construction of daily life, and the ensuing differences in the nature of aging in the United States where social mobility often separates children from their parents and older people are often separated from the large society in age-specific communities. Then the church choir sang a special song for Mr. Lim and attendees sang some of the prepared hymnals.

The event reached its peak when one of Mr. Lim's daughters started the "Happy Birthday" song and a son-in-law offered parents a birthday present—a tour package to Europe. Mr. Lim replied by making a speech and thanked their children and the community members for coming to the celebration. Then entertainment ensued and the celebration began to take on the characteristics of a more ordinary, large community gathering with singing, talking, eating and drinking.

Case 3: The Vietnamese New Year's Day

The *Tet* (short for Tet Nguyen Dan, meaning "festivity on the first morning") or New Year's Day falls on the first day of the lunar calendar (the same as Chinese New Year's Day), and it involves family gatherings to pay respect to their ancestors. The holiday can last for as long as one to three months back in Vietnam. Tet usually demands months of preparation, during which houses are thoroughly cleaned, sometimes even repainted, in order to usher in a brand-new and hopefully lucky year.

The celebration in the United States is abbreviated in many ways, to fit the American work calendar. For example, if Tet falls in the middle of the week, festivities are scheduled for the weekend before and the weekend after Tet. The festivals might include such events as concerts, ballroom dancing, and beauty pageants. For Vietnamese Americans, the celebration of Tet is a way to strengthen cultural values and ties within the community.

The ceremony for the 1994 New Year was held on January 28 at the Asian Social Service Center in South Philadelphia. The Asian Social Service Center, which is affiliated to the St. Thomas Aquinas Church, is a social service organization serving for multi-Asian nationalities in Philadelphia, but their prime clients have been the Southeast Asian population, particularly Vietnamese Americans. Some 1,500 people attended the *Tet* ceremony including those who are not members of the St. Thomas Aquinas Church or the Center. Father Joseph Pham, who is a Vietnamese priest at the Church and director of the Center, reports:

> When we have events or a celebration, people from all over Philadelphia come. Even from Atlantic City or Allentown. At the New Year's celebration, we tried to show second generation kids the good traditions we would like to keep on. We sing a song, had fashion shows, for example, for the younger generation to learn the beauty of Vietnam and the Vietnamese culture. Many people experience an identity crisis. They don't know how to express themselves. They don't know who they are, why they have come here. Through these gatherings and cultural activities, they may realize who they are. (Interview #84)

The Thanksgiving Mass at the St. Thomas Aquinas Church, adjacent to the Center, preceded the actual ceremony. The Mass itself was a mixture of Catholicism and the Vietnamese culture. A lot of attendees were dressed up in Vietnamese traditional costumes, and much of the church rituals were converted into a Thanksgiving ceremony. The cantor, who is also the chair of the organizing committee for the *Tet* ceremony, announced the beginning of the Mass in Vietnamese. Priests and helpers were joined by men and women of all ages, all of whom wore traditional costumes, bringing fresh fruits and harvest gifts. Then they offered these gifts of fruits and vegetables at the altar. Afterwards, all hymns and rituals for the Mass were sung and conducted in Vietnamese. A Vietnamese priest in the rectory emphasized the importance of the *Tet* ceremony for preserving Vietnamese American identity and thanked the rectory for welcoming the Vietnamese population to the church and allowing them to have a ceremony like this. An American priest responded that he was delighted to have Vietnamese Catholics and thanked them for bringing wonderful traditions to enrich the neighborhood. He did not forget to say "Happy New Year!" in Vietnamese at the end. I was genuinely excited to see that many Vietnamese traditions were melded into the church ceremony compared to the Chinese and Korean congregations.

After the Mass, people moved to the Auditorium at the Center where the ancestor worship would be served. On the wall, banners of the Year of Dog and a big map of Vietnam were hung up. At the center of the podium, fresh fruits and foods surrounded the altar. When a drummer signaled the beginning of the ceremony, boys, girls, and men wearing traditional costumes proceeded to the podium with banners. A group of adults who represent the community offered big bows to the altar thanking the ancestors for another prosperous year, then the dragon dance followed. The dragon dance troupe, which is composed of a drummer, a dragon dancer, and a man wearing a mask elevated the mood of the festival and reached high for getting lucky money which was given by Father Joseph Pham. During that time, a torrent of fire crackers released by a group of Vietnamese youths were heard. Kids were lined up to pay respects to the elders and to receive lucky money from community leaders which was wrapped up in red paper bags, inscribed with good wishes and desires for a lucky new year. At the end of the ancestor worship ceremony, a group of youths wearing scouts uniforms wrapped the displayed Vietnamese flag while other attendees sang together the national anthems of Vietnam and the United States.

After the official ceremony, people were divided into two groups: one for enjoying traditional plays and a sing-along at the podium, and another for participating in various traditional games in the basement of the building. Many 1.5 generation Vietnamese American youths entertained with their skills in Vietnamese art and dance. The basement games were mixture of gambling and traditional Vietnamese games, and people were very excited. There was also a bazaar for fundraising.

By this point, the entire building was in a festival mood. The whole event concluded with a dance party.

Case 4: The Chinese New Year Fundraising Dinner

The Annual Chinese New Year Fundraising Dinner sponsored by the Philadelphia Chinatown Development Corporation (PCDC hereafter: details about the organization will be discussed later) is one of the most important events Philadelphia Chinatown can offer. Held in a big banquet room in Chinatown's restaurant, the PCDC, now one of the most powerful key players in Philadelphia Chinatown, invited community leaders within and outside the Chinatown community. More than 30 organizations supported the event including local banks, companies, most of Chinatown's recognized associations and pan-Asian associations in Philadelphia. Since the leadership of the PCDC is composed of American-born generation, people invited at the party were very diverse. By organizing this event, the PCDC not only affirmed the Chinese ethnic identity but demonstrated the sociopolitical recognition in the larger society. The event was publicized to the local media and mayor of Philadelphia stopped by to make a speech. Before the dinner, the event was dominated by a series of speeches given by different political key players in the community. This year's keynote speaker was the Commissioner of Streets of City of Philadelphia, a high-level Chinese American city official. Although the dinner was a Chinese dish and there were Chinese traditional entertainments afterwards, this event was not just a cultural occasion. Through this event, the Chinese assert their identity and show their political influence in the city.

As we see from the above examples, holidays and ethnic traditions are a reaffirmation of community ties and ethnicity. A lot of events are organized by religious organizations or ethnic associations, and the community people are active participants in these events. Somehow these events practiced in the United States serve a more original functions of solidarity than those celebrated at home where the meanings of these events are converted in a secular form (Chin 1991). For Koreans celebrating *Chilsoon*, Chinese gathering at a fundraising banquet, and Vietnamese participating in *Tet* ancestor worship, ethnic traditional events mean the maintaining of cultural identity and the positioning themselves into a strong institution in a multi-racial ethnic landscape. In the United States, ritual events are less frequent, but at the same time the importance of each ritual is much more weighted for both the community at large and for the celebrant.

INTERMARRIAGE

Intermarriage is a good indicator of changes in the nature and perception of ethnic boundaries. Not only does marriage as a culturally patterned institution express traditional beliefs and practices, but it is also one of the main loci through which culture is perpetuated. Whether members of a culture marry within their group or outside of it is a crucial determinant of how the group's boundaries and the strength of its cultural consciousness will be maintained. Marriage also perpetuates culture because it is the basic tie that creates the nuclear family, where socialization takes place and culture is passed from one generation to the next. Thus, marriage is a relationship and an institution that can both reflect and lead change in a society.

From my interview data, several factors were accountable for interracial relationships. The first factor was the environment in which a person grows up, for example, with mixed racial parenthood or in large extended ethnic families. Another factor, which was sometimes correlated with the first factor, was the availability of the people to date or marry. This can be related to urban or suburban upbringing since there is much less ethnic diversity in the suburbs. The third factor was the stereotypes that can play a role in shaping peoples' opinions and helping to continue the existing stereotypes. Finally, in some cases, the interracial relationships was the result of rebellion. Many times children with strict upbringing dated or married colored persons knowing that their parents disapproved.

When asked if they approve or disapprove of intermarriage, what people said and what actually happened were different. Most of my respondents expressed the view that marriage is an individual matter, and they did not seem to care about interracial marriage so long as both parties loved each other. However, very few responded that intermarriages actually happened in their immediate family. Although there are no actual laws today which outlaw interracial relationships, there are still many people who do not believe that mixed couples are normal.

From many of my interviewee's responses, strong in-group marriages were observed. As I have shown before, Chinese parents from Vietnam want their children to marry Chinese. However, intermarriages between Asians are more frequent than interracial marriage, and parents are more tolerant about them. In addition, many of my respondents had experienced dating with other Asians.

Among the younger generation, dating can cause serious problems. The problems are mostly centered on family acceptance of the person who dates. If the person crosses the racial boundaries, he or she sometimes gets a strong reaction from his or her parents. One of my first-generation Chinese American respondents, asked if he would let his children marry a non-Chinese partner, remarked, "I hope they will marry Chinese. I don't want my family to become United Nations" (Interview #41). Some parents explicitly state the preference of marriage partners to their children, and others implicitly force them to consider co-ethnics. Young Min is a second generation Korean American college senior. Her parents do not want her to date anybody other than Koreans. Her father distinctly told her when she was a freshman that he would not talk to her if she dated somebody who is not Korean. Since then, she completely avoided the issue with her father.

> Since my freshmen year when I tried to bring up the guy I date to my parents, it was really difficult. That summer, I hated living at home, because we were still dating, and he [my Caucasian boyfriend] couldn't call my house. I couldn't call him either. The only way I could call him was to go to my best friends' house and use their telephone. Their parents knew it, and I had to pay for the long distance phone bills. It was horrible. I hated it so much. There was a lot of crying, a lot of pain, because I felt like a bad daughter for not telling my parents. But how could I tell that? First, I wasn't sure the relationship was going to last. Second, after my dad told me something like that, how was I supposed to do anything? I felt bad because I felt I wasn't being true to myself. I thought I had to choose between my parents and the guy I met. I sat there and cried, "Why

can't I just be a normal?" But then again, whose definition of normal is it? (Interview #37)

This statement's experience regarding interracial dating is not uncommon among Asian American youths. In a way, such interracial or interethnic clash is also true to most ethnic Americans. What is interesting about Young's statement is how the younger generation Asian Americans interpret their experiences. Torn between two worlds, Young asked a serious questions of what it means to be normal. She asks the same questions that Shawn Chan asked in the previous section about the criteria of "American" identity. Like Shawn, Young is challenging normal/ethnic distinction by implicitly asserting that the American identity is essentially multicultural and therefore that all Americans are ethnic.

ETHNIC ORGANIZATION AND IDENTITY MAKING

In order to understand how a "collective ideology" operates to support the cohesion of an ethnic group, we should understand the ways in which symbols are manipulated by the members of an ethnic collectivity. Individuals differ in their strategies of adaptation, as is reflected in the existence of many organizations and leaders. Much of the everyday lives of families is lived within the boundaries of the social network of family and friends and the church congregation, with little participation in the "wider community."

With a population so residentially and occupationally dispersed, Asian American community institutions are the most visible and permanent identifiers of the presence of an Asian population in Philadelphia. These ethnic associations increase the numbers of Asians actively involved in organizations and increase the number and kinds of activities of Asians in Philadelphia. In a population as dispersed and heterogeneous as the Philadelphia Asians, where a community is defined and manifested in terms of collective public gatherings, ethnic organizations enhance the very existence of the community.

(1) Religious Organizations

Religious organizations are one of the first and principal forms of collective life among immigrants, and are the central symbol of pride and cultural resistance against cultural domination. In this section, I will describe briefly some Chinese and Vietnamese Catholic churches I studied. Then I will provide an analysis of the role of religion in immigrant experiences and discuss the structural complexity of the congregation in Korean Americans churches.

The Chinese American Catholic Church

The Holy Redeemer Church is located on the northern outskirts of Chinatown. The congregation of the church, even among the English speaking group congregation, is primarily composed of Cantonese. However, the church is getting more and more people who speak Mandarin or other Asian languages, such as Laotian and Vietnamese. For example, among seven teenagers baptized in 1993, there were Burmese-, Mandarin-, and other Chinese dialect-speaking youngsters along with Cantonese-speaking members.

The Cantonese group is a heavily Chinatown oriented group. People who live in Chinatown usually come to the Holy Redeemer Church. When people get married and move out to suburbs, they either leave the church or affiliate with local churches in their neighborhood. Because the Holy Redeemer is far from their residence and there are Catholic schools in their neighborhood, most Chinese Americans do not sending their children to the Holy Redeemer. They regularly attend churches in their neighborhood, and only come to the Holy Redeemer occasionally—mostly on holidays. However, they still consider the Holy Redeemer as their church.

The English-speaking mass congregation are mostly teenagers because many of the children who went to the Chinese school at the Holy Redeemer have become Catholic, and continue to come to the mass. The Holy Redeemer plays an important role in introducing them to the Catholic faith and letting them go forward. The church offers Chinese classes for children, as well as Chinese dances and other cultural classes.

The Vietnamese American Catholic Church

In 1976 the Vietnamese Catholic Community in the Archdiocese of Philadelphia was established. The organization has provided religious activities and traditional events for the Vietnamese community. It has also provided support and advice to Vietnamese immigrants and refugees on social adjustments, educated immigrants about naturalization, and helped groups and individuals attain education and employment. In the St. Thomas Aquinas Church in South Philadelphia, one of the bigger Vietnamese Catholic churches in Philadelphia, most of the congregation are recent arrivals or refugees. The rectory is multiethnic, being composed of Vietnamese, Black, Italian, and Irish Americans. Although a mass is conducted in English, there is a Vietnamese mass on Sunday afternoons. About 200 Vietnamese people regularly attend the church. On special occasions like the Christmas mass, however, more than 1500 people attend the events, including people who are not Catholics. The church runs a sister organization called the Asian Social Service Center, which has soon become an integral part of the community. The center operates three nights a week the teaching of English to people of different faiths and nationalities. Currently, four volunteer teachers are teaching about 150 enrolled students. To encourage participation among non-Catholics, the St. Thomas Aquinas also holds various interfaith events.

The St. Alice's church in Upper Darby is another Vietnamese Catholic church in this area. Most of the Vietnamese parishioners are living in Upper Darby. Generally they are better off than those living in South Philadelphia. The church runs the Van Man Center which promotes cultural, spiritual, and social activities for Vietnamese people in this area. Unlike the Asian Social Service Center at the St. Thomas Aquinas, the target group is not the newcomers since most residents in Upper Darby are relatively established. The church is more concerned with helping people find housing, filing applications for public assistance, and connecting Vietnamese with schools and the police department. The Center also runs Vietnamese language classes and organizes cultural activities at Christmas and the New Year. The Center maintains relationship with different agencies in Delaware County such as the Drug and Alcohol Commission. They are also concerned about 1.5 and second generation problems such as high school dropouts, runaway youths, drug abuse, and crime and violence.

The Korean Church as Core Institution
Religious affiliation and people's participation in various organizations are a very distinctive characteristic of Korean Americans. In the Korean

American community Christianity is the majority religion. Other religions, such as Buddhism, are very weak. According to the Philadelphia Buddhist Association, there are American Buddhist centers in University City, South Philadelphia and Center City, and at least three Korean temples scattered around the city. The reason for the small number of Korean Buddhists comes from the scarcity of American temples. While Korean Protestants can rent an American church before they become established, Korean Buddhists cannot obtain spaces because there are very few American Buddhist temples. Often Buddhist congregations start when a group of people begin to gather at someone's home, and members eventually donate enough money to buy a building to serve as a place of worship.

Although Christians only comprise of 25% of the population of Korea, most Korean Americans (70-80%) are Protestant. It is not unusual to hear gospels in many Korean-owned stores and restaurants. The most plausible reason for this prosperity of Christianity among the Korean American community derives from the history of Korean immigration. The early Korean immigrants at the turn of the century were primarily encouraged by American missionaries to come to the United States from Korea. Another reason for the success of Korean American churches is that Christianity tends to promote Americanization by providing institutional contexts to accommodate Korean immigrants to the new environment. As one of my informants mentioned, "if you are not a part of the church, you are not a part of the community." For Koreans, the church community has become the substitute for a territorial ethnic community. It created a certain kind of *Gemeinschaft*, a shared "social world" (Suttles 1968). Susan, a Jewish student, made most of her Korean friends in a local Korean American church. She found an amazing degree of church participation among Korean Americans.

> Immigrant groups tend to become gung-ho religious groups. Koreans seem to take Christianity more seriously than the white majority of Christians. Koreans are really churchgoing, and my friend Hyunjoo has a Jesus picture on the wall. The only Christians I met in high school are Korean. Many Koreans have religious icons in their houses . . . I met a Korean Buddhist family a few years ago, and later on they became Christians. They had a lot of pressure when they first

moved to Cherry Hill. All Koreans living in Cherry Hill are Christians. The lady of the family later said that they just wanted to meet other Korean people. (Interview #13)

Generally immigrant Koreans are sincere Christians. They go on missions not only to Black neighborhood, but even to Africa. One of my interviewees proudly sings Gospel in Swahili, after having served as a missionary doctor in Nigeria. As Dearman (1982) found out from his study of Korean American churches in Los Angeles, most Korean Americans belong to fundamentalist, conservative, or evangelical sects. Minister Cho takes the hardship in Korean immigrant lives as a mission.

America was originally built by sincere and devout Puritans. However, the United States has become corrupted by the evil Satan. It is our God's will that we Koreans re-establish and rescue this promised land from the hands of Satan. God already demonstrated his power by making Korea one of the fastest growing and the most active Christian countries. Pastor Billy Graham once called the success of Christianity in Korea the most miraculous thing that has happened in the twentieth century. Koreans are a truly chosen people. We are led to this land by God's will. (Interview #12)

As we see from the above, strong Christian values and morals lead Korean Americans to perceive that their hardship is God's will and it is their mission to revitalize American society. Here, the notion of a diaspora is invested with religious meaning and the Korean American identity feeds upon this religious discourse.

Not only does the church dominate Korean immigrant life generally, but being Christian also affected the way individual Korean immigrants responded to discrimination by white Americans. They often compare the discrimination and the lack of opportunity experienced in Korea with that of the United States. Since most East Asian countries have imposed very strict regulations toward aliens, most first-generation Korean American professionals take the American dream and believe that the American society provides fair opportunities. We find this type of religious rhetoric from the early Korean immigrant experiences.

I asked Father why we had to come to a place where we were not wanted. He replied that we deserved what we got because that was the same kind of treatment that Koreans had given to the first American missionaries in Korea (May Paik Lee, *Quiet Odyssey*, p. 12)

According to the *Directory of the Korean Church in Greater Philadelphia (1990)*, there are 99 Korean Protestant churches in the Philadelphia area. The oldest Korean church in Philadelphia was founded in 1952, however, most churches were established after 1980 when the Korean population grew very quickly in this area. In the 1950's there was only one church in this area. From 1960-69, there were two more churches. In the 1970's, 26 churches were established. In the 1980's 60 churches opened. Among them, the Presbyterian Church is by far dominant (53%), followed by Methodist (11%), Baptist (6%), and others (29%).

A large percentage of American Presbyterians and Methodists are relatively well-educated, but the educational level of those who belong to the Pentecostal type of denominations like the Church of God and Assembly of God is in general lower than the former. Most intellectuals who belong to the former type of the church have a tendency to prefer a quiet, reverent worship service, while those who belong to the latter type of churches have a tendency to prefer an emotional worship service (Kim 1991). It appears that Korean American churches do not maintain a strong stance on issues of racial oppression, discrimination, or ethnic prejudice. They are generally not concerned with active social and political movements.

A closer look at the phenomenal increase of the Korean American churches allows us to find a prevailing schismatic tendency among ethnic churches. This tendency to schism, accompanied by an abundant supply of Korean ministers, has caused a fierce inter-church competition in recruiting church members in the immigrant communities (Shin and Park 1988). Each year, as I have observed, about two or three churches split from larger churches in the Philadelphia area. There exists a severe entrepreneurial competition among these religious denominations, and a strong tendency among Korean Americans toward the competitive and mutually exclusive "my-church-ism" adherence.

Church X: A Case

One of the oldest and the largest Korean churches in Philadelphia is located on the 48th and Spruce Street. The church extends its history to 1971 when they shared the building with an American church on 37th and Chestnut Street. In 1980, they bought a building and established their own church. Now the church boasts more than 500 congregation ,members from Philadelphia, New Jersey, and Delaware.

Sunday church services are usually conducted both in Korean and in English at separate times. Like other Korean churches, this church has more than one Sunday service. On Saturday the church operates a Korean school. It is a service to this region, and the students of this school are not necessarily church members. There are about 110 students in this school, and 50% are not members of this church. The church has two school buses; however, some parents organized a car pool. Besides the Korean language, the school has classes on Korean song, dance, fine arts, calligraphy, and *Taekwondo* (martial arts). Teachers are recruited among graduate students at nearby universities.

In this church, Christian holidays are observed seriously. However, most Korean traditional holidays have faded away, and if ever observed, they are done so by individual families. For example, *Chusok*, one of the biggest holidays in Korea is sometimes observed on Thanksgivings Day. Other than holidays, many church members go to the annual *Sooyanghoe* (a religious summer camp) during the summer, and the annual picnic to Ridley Creek Park on Memorial Day.

There are many associations within this church based on age and sex. These associations are operated autonomously. They have their own officers, presidents, and these people are independently elected by its members. The Women's Evangelical Association and the Men's Evangelical Association form the core organizations among members. The young men's Association is divided into three sub-organizations. Married graduate students form one group, single Korean-speaking college students form another group, and single English-speaking students have their own group. The basic activities of these groups are Bible meetings, outings, and missionary services to both the American and Korean community.

There are also associations of the second generation students. These are (1) A High School Association (every Friday)- Bible study.

(2) Undergraduate Association (every Saturday morning)- Bible meeting, fellowship, service and mission. These groups are very actively engaged in fundamental evangelism. During the church's main evangelical activities, called "Evangelical Explosive," these groups reached out to various individuals and neighborhoods every Tuesday and Saturday. The association for seniors (*Somanghoe*) made kimchi and sold it to the grocery store to contribute money to enlarge the parking lot of the church.

There are also an organization of churches and an association of pastors in the Philadelphia area. The committee was constituted 10 years ago. The church committee organizes interchurch activities such as the Korean-Black united congregations. Koreans and Black Americans visit either church for Sunday service, and after the service they get together and talk. Food is usually prepared by each church's members in turn. At a recent congregation, about 300 Koreans and 300 Blacks gathered. Korean and black ministers gave their sermons for 15 minutes each. United choirs sang gospel together. And then there were welcoming addresses and fellowships. That was the only united congregation which Koreans shared with other ethnic groups.

The committee promotes united services at Christmas and Easter. At Easter, Koreans gather at 6 a.m. in front of the Philadelphia Art Museum. On New Year's Day, they have a breakfast prayer meeting. They also have a united service on August 15 (Liberation Day from Japanese Colonial Rule: the same as V-Day). In September, Koreans have an evangelical meeting in this region. Some outside lecturers from both Korea and America come and give lectures.

The church is administratively composed of the Governing Body, the Operating Body (deacon), and the Board of Trustees. In the church where I conducted my fieldwork there are nine *jangro* (elders), four *jeondosa* (evangelists), and two *kangdosa* (preachers who will become pastors). There are 60-70 *jipsa* (deacons and deaconesses) in this church. Among elders, three of them are from the business class, while the rest of them are professionals. There are about thirty-five professionals among the deacons.

The congregation uses the minister's nonreligious activity as the main criterion for judging him. Thus organizational executive ability in operating church programs constitutes the highest quality of a minister. Usually, church programs have become a source of interchurch competition for membership and prestige. In their nonreligious roles, churches act as brokers between Korean immigrants and the dominant institutions of the larger society. Minister Cho in the Church X tells me about extra-church affairs he has to handle in Korean American churches.

> To be a minister in a Korean American church is very difficult. If I hear about someone coming from Korea, I have to pick them up at the airport. If they do not know how to start their life here, I have to introduce them to one of our church members for help. If they encounter some serious problems such as legal problems, I have to defend them in court. Here, ministers take care of all their members, and people take it for granted. (Interview #12)

One of the most unique characteristics of the Korean American church is the number of church laymen and the structure. Min's (1991) survey of Korean American churches in New York City shows that the churches have on average 78.5 lay officers out of 248 congregation members (about a third). Korean immigrants' lack of fulfillment in their social integration in the larger American society makes the holding of church offices (elders, deacons, etc.) very important to them. People are usually addressed as "Mr. Deacon" or "Mr. Elder" in almost all social situations once they obtain the lay leadership. Cliques and factions form within a congregation on the basis of shared interests and background. Those who fail to get elected to the lay leadership positions frequently opt to lead their supporters in establishing a new church where they can be elected to the leadership position without any opposition. Together with individuals' eagerness to accept the lay leadership positions to enhance their marginal status, this competition eventually leads to schism. Mr. Lee, a first-generation small business owner, tells me about his congregation.

> Within my church, we have groups of doctors, lawyers, students, and of course, "ordinary people." I think their [professionals'] boundary maintenance is much more intense than in Korea. They have different life styles and different social gatherings. I feel distinctive lines between these groups. In some churches, certain groups dominate, and in other churches, they are mixed, but with a clear distinction. It

is a very natural phenomenon or process in Korean churches here. For example, the church I belong to is composed of 90% working or small business classes. On the other hand, in another church, most members are doctors and lawyers. (Interview #1)

As one of my interviewees indicated above, there are certain processes going on; the homogenization within church congregations and the differentiation among churches. In addition to the obsession toward church lay leadership among Korean Americans, the reason for this process can be derived from the very notion of religion itself.

It is often argued that Korean religions in general strongly reflect Koreans' eagerness to make their lives better. Korean indigenous religions—almost all of different sorts—focus on success in this world, as opposed to Christianity's focus on the other world. Koreans traditionally had no idea of "Original Sin," a core concept of the Christianity. Koreans are believed to be more concerned with their existential problems in this world, and thus accommodate elements of various religions without any serious inner conflict as indicated in the following interview:

I was a Christian in Korea. My mother changed her religious affiliation because it helped to accomplish her wishes. My mother's wish was to come to the United States, so she married my father [an American GI]. But for some reason, she could not make it. One day, her friend suggested that she attend the [Buddhist] Temple and pray there for three months, and then her wish would come true. So she and I started to go to the temple. After that, she indeed made me come here, and since I obtained citizenship, I can invite her. She finally realized her wish, and she is coming next year. I go to the Center [Temple] five times, sometimes seven times, a week whenever a meeting is held. I spend 3 to 4 hours a day there. So I spend approximately 25 hours in a week [at the Center], and that is my whole social life other than my job at the bank. (Interview #5)

Those who do make it in the United States strengthen their ties and solidarity by recruiting friends and relatives and colleagues into the same church. When I attended a fundraising dinner banquet for initiating a Korean Studies Program at the University of Pennsylvania which was sponsored by rich Korean American businessmen and professionals, the meeting started with a blessing by a minister from one of the biggest churches in Philadelphia, which is largely composed of an upper-middle class congregation.

In a similar way, those who have not succeeded in immigrant life experience a heavy moral burden and a sense of inferiority and thus are gradually driven out of the church. Mr. Lee (Interview #1) had mentioned that he didn't feel comfortable attending the bigger church, and recently joined another small church. Small churches usually fulfill the immediate needs of their homogeneous "clients," and members of the working-class and less fortunate businessmen share the "hinterland cultures." In the case of Korean Americans, class may be a clear indicator for differentiation of churches.

A district service enhances this differentiation process. About once a month, Korean church members who live near each other form a block meeting where people study the Bible and talk over religious subjects. The service is usually led by lay members of the church. The purpose of the district service area is to promote mutual assistance among nearby members and enhance their faith by holding a religious service at a member's residence on a rotational basis. However, the district service strongly enhances the attachment of people from the same groupings. Very frequently, *kye* (the rotating credit association) is practiced among members of district services.

However, most second generation Korean Americans do not share the same understanding of Christianity—the Korean Protestant means something different to them. They do not subscribe to the first generation Korean American Christianity. The important function of the church besides faith has been to help Koreans maintain their identity. Sometimes you wonder what comes first, Jesus Christ or the culture. Michael Kang, a second generation Korean American, describes the different perceptions about Korean American Christianity between first- and second-generations.

> Though my parents are Christian, I still wonder whether their Christianity is dominant or whether their "Koreanness" is. I am unsure of what God wants me to do in the future and I have told my parents that I am considering both teaching at a high school in the States or going overseas to work as a missionary or a pastor. My

father's immediate reply was his desire for me to stay and he reminded me that I was his only son. I struggled with my desire to honor my parents, but my first love is to Christ. My parents had dealt fairly well with my earlier desires to be a teacher, though as most Asian parents they wanted me to be a doctor, a businessman, or a lawyer. Now after getting used to the idea of me teaching, they are faced with another challenge. I feel that there is a generation gap between first generation Korean Christianity and my Christianity as a second generation Korean. I wonder what exactly is preached when my parents go to Korean church service and whether Korean Christian culture has shrouded the true meaning of Christ's death on the cross and His Lordship. (Interview #71)

Second generation Korean Americans criticize the Korean churches for being self-serving and parochial especially when it comes to inter-racial relationships. Korean churches provide their resources to only fellow Koreans, but not to other members of the community. The church may foster a feeling of ethnocentrism and it is contradictory to the teachings of Christ, they say. They believe what holds the first generation Korean church members together is the "Koreanness," not Christianity. Second generation Korean Americans in various instances try to reconcile Koreanness with their Christian faith.

(2) *Voluntary Associations*

Asian Americans, although claimed as being economically successful, have not been socially integrated into the mainstream society. They might operate extensive informal mutual help organizations, but the organizational penetration has not reached into the major educational, occupational, or political institutions of the society. They have not yet been successful in participating in the social cliques and clubs that lead to intimate primary relationships. In other words, they lack "the old boy network." As Bourdieu (1984) argues, this is a significant area for capitalizing on cultural resources.

The reason for the lack of participation in the mainstream associations is derived from the strong presence of the immigrant generation in this area. Most immigrants are busy establishing themselves and there is simply no time to devote to other social lives.

However, the reason also comes from the notion of "economic stability first,"—the different strategy from what other ethnic groups stressed, such as the Irish for politics and the Blacks for the campaign against racial injustices—among many Asian immigrant families. To meet these ends, Asian Americans have developed numerous ethnic-based mutual assistance associations.

Chinatown: The Contending Organizations

In the United States, different types of organizations were established in response to the growing and neglected needs of the Chinese American community. These included education groups (i.e. Chinese schools) based on the Chinese-teaching ideal, clans based on family name, "Hui Kuans (會館)" based on district or dialect, "Tangs (堂)" based on personal interests, and merchant associations based on business interests. Before the recent Mandarin immigration and Chinese dispersion into suburbs, these organizations were powerful, handling important matters such as language learning, business affairs, family or personal disputes and immigration problems. They operated under the umbrella of the Chinese Benevolent Association (CBA), which was the supreme power (Chen 1992). However, as the Chinese community has grown, their assumed superiority has been challenged by younger generations. The following interview segment told by Lei Lu shows that the two organizations differ not only in composition of their members but also in their procedures and techniques of dealing with the dominant society.

> In Chinatown, there are two most important associations. One is the PCDC [Philadelphia Chinatown Development Corporation] and the other is the CBA [Chinese Benevolent Association]. PCDC people cannot speak Chinese. They are born here, and they forgot Chinese. They are, what we call, ABC [American Born Chinese]. They recognize Chinatown as very important. They can speak beautiful English. So they know how to play games with the city hall. The other one is CBA. The members of CBA speak Chinese, especially Cantonese and English. But they are traditional. They are the leaders who organize celebrations like the Chinese New Year and the National Day of Taiwan. Because they are bilingual, they have some programs like an English class to help new immigrants. CBA are the first generation, but they came here a long time ago. They are old.

Most of the leaders are 60 years old. More than 60. These two groups just reflect the very interesting aspects about the generation gap. So sometimes conflict arises. They all like Chinatown, but when they are doing something, maybe arguing with the city hall, their methods are totally different. The PCDC fights, argues, in an American style. But the other [the CBA] is very humble, people just visit the city hall, write letters. The PCDC goes to TV station, argues, fights, it's very different. So it's very interesting. But they all like Chinatown. (Interview #41)

A second-generation Chinese American social worker notes the different approaches this way.

First generation, especially older generation, the way they outlook, they feel like they do not belong here. They still hold a kind of a sojourner mentality that they are guests in this country. They don't want to be up in the front in fighting. (Interview #86)

The second-generation Chinese Americans identify the CBA as being primarily composed of first-generationers. They criticize the CBA for being more concerned with home affairs rather than community affairs in the United States.

The Chinese Benevolent Association (CBA)

The Chinese Benevolent Association is composed of 10 member organizations, which can be variously categorized as regional or dialectal organizations, clan organizations, chambers of commerce, cultural organizations and educational groups. Each member organization performs its activities separately. The members of the umbrella association are mostly China-born immigrants who came to this country many years ago, and they are entrepreneurs in typically Chinese businesses in Chinatown. To them, serving as officers in the various traditional associations can bring both prestige and a solid following. Their many years of residence in the United States have brought some practical knowledge about this country, and thus they are familiar with two cultural systems—Chinese and American. CBA members are primarily interested in maintaining and displaying

"Chineseness" through traditional festivals and by involving themselves in the affairs of the associations.

The CBA was not adequately prepared to tackle the contemporary social problems of the new immigrants, such as housing, medicare, employment, and youth problems. To them, an ethnic group is a unit of cultural transmission. The common responsibility of member organizations of the CBA is to donate money to the fund of the CBA on the Chinese New Year or to support the activities initiated by this association, for example, the parade on the National Day and the feast at the Chinese New Year Festival.

The Chinese from Vietnam have formed their own organization, the Overseas Chinese Association of Greater Philadelphia. "They [Overseas Chinese Association] respect the CBA a lot, like their boss in Chinatown," Lei Lu continues, "but they are outside of the Chinatown organization. They don't work together often" (Interview #41). It is apparent that the Chinese Vietnamese population, although increasingly being incorporated into a bigger Chinese American community, is quite separated in terms of their organizational life.

The Philadelphia Chinatown Development Corporation (PCDC)

The prime contender organization of the CBA in Philadelphia Chinatown is the Philadelphia Chinatown Development Corporation (PCDC). The PCDC is a grassroots non-profit organization which works to upgrade the living standards of the Chinese community. The organization was established in response to the original proposal for the widening of the Vine Street Expressway which would have demolished the Holy Redeemer Catholic Church and School and severely disrupted other aspects of life in Chinatown. The Chinatown community became concerned and the first town meeting was called in response to the Vine Street proposal in 1966. Three years later the committee was incorporated as the Philadelphia Chinatown Development Corporation (PCDC). Since it has been established at the danger of eliminating identity by outside forces, it has become a major institution to assert their identity through physical architecture.

Since its inception, the PCDC has broadened its scope of service to include housing developments for families and the elderly, site improvements, and community planning for the residents in Philadelphia Chinatown. In addition to successfully blocking the original Vine Street Expressway proposal and in helping to redesign the final approved proposal of the Expressway, the PCDC also participated in the city's decision to construct the noise walls along the Vine Street and in their ultimate design. It should be obvious that the PCDC's goals are "not only to maintain Chinatown as a visible ethnic community in a literal, physical level but also to enable the Chinese Americans who inhabit Chinatown to express their heritage on a cultural level" (Butcher 1990). In a way, the PCDC has played a role as an agent for change and a culture broker between the Chinese subculture and the American culture, a mediator between the community and the city.

The membership of the PCDC is mostly composed of American-born Chinese professionals who are employed in American establishments as well as in Chinatown, and thus they are more familiar with the English language and American society. As educated individuals, PCDC members understand how to work with the dominant society and its institutions to help the Chinese American community. The PCDC knows how to deal with the mainstream society, such as city governments, and its members share a political perspective that considers the pursuit of political empowerment as an inherent feature of a democratic plural society. To members of the PCDC, the ethnic group is used not principally as a carrier of cultural traditions, but as an interest or pressure group for political and economic activities. To meet these ends, the PCDC sometimes utilizes a larger ethnic identity—Asian American, and forms coalitions with other Asians for the attainment of similar institutional goals.

Due to the differences in language, life-styles, and mentality, there has been little interaction between the new elite and the traditional elite. Some conflicts and attacks on each other have been frequent. As one of the older generation Chinese Americans told me, "I don't understand how those young American-born Chinese identify themselves as Chinese or Asian despite the fact that they cannot speak Chinese and know nothing about the Chinese culture." PCDC people, on the other hand, charge the traditional leaders for being not concerned with the needs of the ordinary Chinese, but rather with the needs of business and employers in Chinatown. They believe that they are more equipped with the methods for tapping the resources of the larger society and for dealing with American politics. Li-chiu mentions the struggle in this way.

> I think sometimes there are culture disputes. There is more of a man-dominating atmosphere at CBA. They still keep that as a culture. Cynthia is probably the first woman ever elected to be on their board. But she was there for only a year. I don't think there will be ever another female to be on their board. (Interview #46)

The rivalry between the CBA and the PCDC is not confined to the organizational level. It is rather derived from a more fundamental difference; a contrasting definition of Chinese Americanness, a different set of assumptions, attitudes, and behaviors, or a different "culture."

The Asian Americans United (AAU)

Besides community-based organizations that delivered direct services to a physical community such as Chinatown, there are alternative grassroots organizations identified with the larger Asian American community. The Asian Americans United, which is located at 8th and Arch Streets, provides tutoring and other services for poor and working-class Asian Americans. They are more connected with the grassroots population in Asian American communities. Their activities include the Community Youth Leadership Project, in which Asian American youths run an after-school tutorial program for Asian immigrant children. These youths participate in workshops focusing on issues in the community and develop a project centered around these issues. The active members of the AAU are primarily second generation Asian Americans, particularly Chinese Americans. They target low-income Asians who are disenfranchised. Even though the AAU is located near Chinatown, they have never had a strong relationship with Chinatown until 1992.

The relationship began to strengthen after they ran a summer program, hiring some high school youths to be tutors or mentors for elementary school children and offered leadership training for community work. The AAU also organized a meeting between Asian parents and the School Board members at the Chinese Christian Church to bring up their concerns such as hiring Asian bilingual teachers. The

AAU has previously held similar programs with the Vietnamese, Cambodian, and Lao communities in West Philadelphia before they initiated the program in Chinatown. After the summer program, the AAU organized Chinese residents in Chinatown for obtaining school bus service for Chinatown kids. When they worked with Chinatown, according to the director of the AAU, the Chinese Christian Center was most helpful to organize residents. However, there has been a minimal contact with the CBA.

The AAU works very much in an American way. Since 1991, the AAU has been producing Asian American communities segments of the "Community Forum" for a local TV station. The show is live once a week and presents viewpoints and issues from Philadelphia's many minority communities, and the AAU's segments appear once a month. For example, in December 1993, there was a show on tensions between Korean merchants and African American communities featuring live guests from both communities talking about their efforts to bridge gaps in their communities. Steve Kuo, an officer at the AAU describes how first-generation Chinese residents perceive the organization.

> When we plan rallies or demonstrations, we send all relevant information to all local newspapers and TV stations. We try to get as much coverage as we can. One criticism we get back from all these activities is that we are too American. We do things too much in an American way. (Interview #86)

However, the contention between these conflicting organizations is inevitable given the changing structure of the Philadelphia Chinese community, and it is not an entirely undesirable phenomenon. Rather, the different usage of ethnicity—the CBA for assisting members of the community to participate in the social, economic, and political life in Philadelphia Chinatown, whereas the PCDC for obtaining funding from city, state, and federal governments and for gaining employment and financial aid for the Chinese—provides us with a more complete and dynamic picture of the community-making in process.

Proliferation of Organization by Koreans

It is interesting to investigate how Korean Americans with different educational and class backgrounds view themselves vis-a-vis the wider society. Subjective feelings of ethnic group or racial identification may be a more powerful determinant of behavior. The increasing differentiation within the Korean American community tends to lengthen the social and psychological distance between the community's professionals, small business entrepreneurs, and working class residents by differentiating the institutional contexts in which the interests of the three groups were articulated and addressed. The polarization of interests among the community's organizations gave institutional form to class divisions in the community. For example, to many professional organizations such as the Korean American Professional Association (KAPA) and the Korean Women's Association, a good education (usually elite education) and a good location for a high school are the main issues. Entrepreneurs form the Korean Business Association, which was established in 1974, or the numerous different business associations such as the Korean Laundry Association. Only the working class lacks the organizational bases to represent their interests.

Patterns of differential associations among Korean immigrants have emerged in the immigrant community on the basis of such characteristics as duration of residence in the United States, province of origin in Korea, high school/college alumni ties, political orientations, and they are closely related to the rotating credit association (*kye*, 계). *Kye* is an established institution among Korean Americans in which persons who know and trust one another and who want to secure a loan each contribute a set sum of money on a regular basis, which then is deposited or invested so as to gain a favorable rate of interest. At prescribed intervals, each member receives a set amount of money from the pool and, thereafter, pays interest on the loan he has received. The fund is replenished by the regular contributions of the members, the interest that the pool itself is earning, and the interest that is paid in by the loan recipients. According to my interview data among Korean Americans, about 60% of Koreans practice *kye*. *Kye* is a good source for either consumption or investment. The small business class strongly uses *kye* as a financial resource, whereas professionals don't practice *kye* much. My findings are contradictory with Kennedy's (1973) findings that Koreans with higher education and income are more likely to belong to *kye* than lower status persons. However, it should be noted that even though professionals themselves are not engaged in *kye*, it is highly likely that their spouses or some family members are participating in it. For example, wives of my male informants usually have their own small stores, and they often draw some money from *kye*. On the other hand, the main reason for working class people who do not practice *kye* is that they do not earn enough money for it, rather than that they oppose it. Therefore, *kye* is a common resource of finance, at least for the business class, and quite a popular private association among Korean Americans.

While a number of scholars have looked at *kye* from different angles (Ardener 1964; Geertz 1962; Kennedy 1973; Kim 1982; Light and others 1990), I was most interested in the membership of the *kye*. Who are the members? Who is included and who is not? *Kye* is not only an economic institution but a social institution. Once this type of association is formed, the members consider themselves as peers. Class identification is also expressed in patterns of neighborhood preference. Like other middle-class groups Korean Americans tend to associate with people from their own stratum. I observed that middle class Korean American professionals had a relatively extensive friendship network which ranged across all occupational statuses, while persons of lower socio-economic status tended to have had friendships with persons closer to their own occupational status. Most *kye* members, in fact, are recruited through existing members' personal networks, and usually within the same socio-economic background.

Korean ethnic professionals organize their own cliques like law agencies (for example, the Asian American Law Center), doctors' associations (for instance, the Korean American Medical Doctor's Association), or service institutions like the Philip Jaisohn Foundation which primarily reach out to larger communities. The Korean Community Development Services Center, led by a Korean American doctor, provides comprehensive direct services for newly arrived Asian immigrants and refugees as well as other minority group members. Growing out of a social service organization from Korean Business Association, the Center is now serving other Asian Americans as well, particularly the Southeast Asian population in the Northeast section. The Center's services include employment and training programs; programs for the elderly; basic English education for adults; health care for those with no health care provisions; and free initial legal consultation. The Center has worked with various Asian groups on special projects, such as a soccer tournament for Southeast Asian youth.

Korean American professionals are in a way middlemen between the societies. Often, the ethnic professionals have to deal with the dialogue between the Korean American community and the homeland government. Korean American professionals have become more and more engaged in community affairs as mediators. Although they have been relatively successful in accommodating themselves to American society, they are not yet fully incorporated into the mainstream. Most Korean American doctors live in nice neighborhoods, which provide a good education for their children. They have "made it," at least economically speaking. However, as I have demonstrated above through a description of their networks and organizational lives, they are socially still ethnic. Some recently-immigrated Korean American workers and businessmen blame Korean American professionals (including doctors) for not participating enough in community activities. However, it is the ethnic professionals who have the connections and knowledge to publicize and relate the community issues to the larger society.

The small business class can become rich and established, yet they seldom move to the mainstream market. The best possible way to gain prestige equivalent to the mainstream acceptance has been through participating in ethnic organizations and through becoming a leader. Although the Korean Association in Philadelphia was started by a handful of students at the University of Pennsylvania, the leadership has gradually moved into the hands of small business owners.

The Korean Association is hierarchical; the President is expected to be the spokesperson for the entire Korean population. While officers of the Korean Association is recognized by the city establishment, many of the grassroots Korean American population are not linked to such leadership. For example, Korean American political organizations receive little recognition and support from well-educated, professional Korean Americans. They are relatively less likely to take an active role in politics. It is usually the case that upwardly mobile individuals are less likely to identify with the Korean American subculture and, hence, with ethnically based organizations.

I am sick and tired of the Korean Association of Philadelphia. They
are not a true representative of the Korean community. Most of the
officers there spend time and energy on their own private matters.
They are rich businessmen. They want to get *gamtu* [Korean:
prestigious positions] through participating in it. The Association
maintains hierarchical structures and its officers behave in a
bureaucratic way just like Korean government officials do. I think
most Koreans here don't know what they are doing. They don't even
care. (Interview #34)

Few Korean Americans know of the activities of the Korean
Association or the officers of the organization. Many Koreans do not
approve of their activities. The Philadelphia Korean population is
internally fragmented yet externally conceived of as homogeneous.
There is therefore a struggle between the internal segments to represent
the community as a whole. The "community" is represented by
opposed elites competing for local hegemony. Thus, when a Korean
American ran at the primary election of the City Council of
Philadelphia in 1991, the Korean Association did not endorse him, and
many ethnic associations just split over the support of a candidate.
People argued over the "representativeness" of him as a Korean
American. He was never regarded as an individual, only as the first
Korean to run for city office. He owns a martial art studio in Northeast
Philadelphia.

Is there no influence, then, from ethnic networking to help the
second generation to get into the primary sector? This question is worth
investigating. Second generation Koreans are also interested in their
homeland politics and culture. When Korea became important in the
world economy, more and more Korean students went to Korea over
the summer vacation, and learned the Korean language and about
Korean culture (Bond 1990). Many students these days hope to relate
their cultural heritage to their future career. There are many
organizations for Korean American college students, and they are
active in both Korean and Korean American communities. One of the
distinctive organizations is Young Koreans United (YKU). The
members of YKU are United States-educated Korean Americans who
integrate partial concerns about their new land with those about the

homeland. As Chang (1988) and Park (1991) described it, they can be a major interest group within Korean American political structure.

Vietnamese Americans and Service Agencies

Unlike Chinese and Korean Americans, there are few class distinctions in the Vietnamese American community. Most of them retain lower- or lower middle-class occupations, and many arrived in the United States as refugees. The distinguishing characteristic of the contemporary refugee experience is the federal system which has been created to regulate and aid the flow of entering refugees. In Philadelphia, four volunteer agencies are assisting Southeast Asian refugees including Vietnamese: the Nationality Service Center, Jewish Vocational Services, the Lutheran Children and Family Service, and Catholic Social Services. The initial experience of the Vietnamese with the government refugee apparatus may have eased the incorporation of the public assistance system into the coping strategies constructed by the group. In addition, the government system has had an impact on the formal Vietnamese ethnic community structure. The growth of the Vietnamese ethnic organizations had been encouraged in certain ways by the state "refugee bureaucracy." But the government system has also influenced the ethnic associations' patterns of development in a fashion that furthered the historically rooted distance and animosity felt by most Vietnamese Americans towards formal ethnic organizations. Dr. Tran explains the lack of voluntary associations in Vietnamese American community in this way.

> The Korean community is an immigrant community, so they [the Koreans] are much more prepared. They know what they want to do; study, do business. The Vietnamese community is completely different in a sense that they are forced to be here. They are not prepared. They have to spend a lot of time just for survival. And that's very hard. When you are prepared to go to another country, you already know something about the country, what you can do in order to survive. People coming here just don't have any idea, they are just thrown into the place. Economic survival is something which really preoccupies everybody. In order to set up an agency in the United States, you have to have an entrepreneurial spirit in order to make it survive. Here what most Vietnamese people want to do is so-called mutual assistance. They don't know the entrepreneurial spirit of how

to organize associations. If they want to do something, they set up in their own house in their spare time, and sooner or later, they get exhausted. And people around them become suspicious about whether they make money out of this. And for all of these reasons, the religious organizations survived. (Interview #60)

Thus with a very low level of community organizational support and the dislocation of family members, the newly arriving Vietnamese had to establish themselves independently in the community. Naturally, the family has become the single most important institution for contributing a household economy among Vietnamese Americans. Economic survival is very important not only for Vietnamese individuals themselves but for family members whom they try to bring over to the United States. Parishes and church congregations, local social service agencies, and American families who sponsored Vietnamese refugees were all instrumental in helping many Vietnamese to develop networks from the ground up. Although they do have the Vietnamese United National Association—a sort of umbrella organization like the Korean Association of the Greater Philadelphia— its activities have been minimal, and many of my interviewees did not feel a strong affiliation to it.

ETHNIC MEDIA

By informing geographically dispersed immigrants of community meetings and events, the media are a most powerful means of integrating and sustaining them. Most first generation immigrants subscribe to ethnic newspapers and regularly watch TV programs or video tapes from their home country. The papers are distributed through newsstands and selected bookstores, groceries, or some ethnic restaurants. Ethnic media inform immigrants about events that have taken place within and outside their community and about available social services. These media also offer an easy source through which older immigrants can maintain a stabilizing continuity in their cultural and entertainment life and younger immigrants can maintain contact with their roots (Lum 1991). Ethnic media shape opinions, and link ethnic communities in different regions together.

Chinese American Newspaper

There are two major Chinese newspapers circulated in the Philadelphia area. The older one is the *World Journal* (世界日報). It is a sister newspaper of the United Daily News (UDN) in Taipei, an independent Chinese language newspaper registered in North America. The UDN has a number of corporate affiliated newspapers. The first issue of the *World Journal* appeared in New York and San Francisco in 1976. This daily newspaper offers a full range of news, including international, national, and local Chinese community items. The first three pages are devoted to events in the United States and the world. Then two pages are reserved for news about Hong Kong. Because this newspaper's headquarters are in Taipei, three pages are devoted to Taiwanese news. Then there are two pages of mainland China news. Other pages are devoted to economic news in Taiwan and Hong Kong, and economic sections from mainland China. The rest of the newspaper is for the local news of the Delaware valley. Other sections include editorials and opinion; cultural and entertainment activities; social news, family affairs, advice columns; and advertisements. The *World Journal* has a news coverage network in the United States and Canada, with its correspondents stationed in major metropolitan areas. There are reporters in different cities around the country. In New York there are ten news reporters, but in Philadelphia there is only one. The Philadelphia reporter writes news for the local news section and sends them to the headquarters. Then the major news pages prepared in New York are transmitted via satellite for publication in San Francisco.

Korean American Newspaper

During the Summer Olympic Games in 1988, many Korean immigrants watched Olympic updates from Korean news broadcasts via satellite, rather than from American networks. As of now, there are five Korean-language daily newspapers thriving and competing for readership, and more than 80 percent of Koreans locally read Korean-language newspapers instead of English-language daily newspapers.

For example, in *Joong-Ang Ilbo* (중앙일보), reporters cover the community from a makeshift office inside a Korean shopping complex on Cheltenham Avenue that also houses a broadcasting studio. Like other competing newspapers, the office is independently owned and operated, but is affiliated with the *Joong-Ang Ilbo* in South Korea. Reporters fax local news to the U.S. headquarters of the *Joong-Ang Ilbo* in New York, where a larger staff pastes the local articles alongside national and international news received from the home office and prints the newspapers. *Dong-a Ilbo* (동아일보) is the only major Korean newspaper locally published in Philadelphia. Like most of the five dailies, the *Dong-a Ilbo* is planning to publish an English-language supplement to attract second-generation Koreans.

Also to be noted is the proliferation of small tabloid newspapers and newsletters from business associations. They are published once a week, and carry more information about the Korean community in Philadelphia, including the job information. One of the important features in these newsletters is a cartoon series about a Korean American small business owner. The cartoon depicts the hardship of living in the United States as an immigrant, and provides wisdom and tips arising from those experiences. Most of the time it carries a heavy religious tone and Korean nationalistic ideology.

Vietnamese Americans

Like the Chinese and the Koreans, the Vietnamese community produces several community newspapers, which depend on local advertisements. Some of them propagate political ideas. One or two national newspapers are published in California. There is a Vietnamese radio station in San Jose, and a news video station in Houston. Every Sunday Vietnamese Americans can watch the news imported from these headquarters.

The major media-based form of entertainment in the life of the average Korean and Vietnamese in Philadelphia is watching video tapes. Vietnamese prefer videos produced in Hong Kong and Taiwan and are therefore familiar with the movies and TV stars in Hong Kong and Taiwan. There are some Vietnamese-language videos made in Vietnam, but the quality is judged inferior to those produced in Hong Kong and Taiwan. Recently, some Vietnamese stars visited the United Sates to make their own videos for the Vietnamese American audience. Many music videos or soap operas are produced in California.

Many first generation immigrants rely on the community media for vital information necessary for their daily living. For them, the community media are the only source of pleasure, comfort, information, and education. Usually there are some sections of local news and advertising. Advertisers in newspapers can influence the reporting of stories, and I heard occasionally of the acceptance of a bribe by these newspaper owners. Often these newspaper companies are owned by rich businessmen, and their interpretation of issues and events tends to be somewhat parochial. Secondly it is fair to say that the reporters and editors are not sufficiently professionalized. Sometimes ethnic media are heavily homeland-oriented, reflecting the perspectives and interests of the first generation immigrants.

ELECTORAL POLITICS AND BEYOND

Roberto Unger defines politics as "struggle over the resources and arrangements that set the basic terms of our practical and passionate relations" (Unger 1987). Preeminent among these arrangements, he observes, is the formative institutional and imaginative contexts of social life. Politics in this sense concerns all aspects of institutional organization, public action, social practices and habits, and cultural meanings insofar as they are potentially subject to collective evaluation and decision making (Young 1990).

The presumed apolitical character of Asian Americans derives from the misconception that electoral participation is the sole important criterion for the political participation. The UCLA Asian Pacific American Registration Study found that 43 percent of Japanese Americans, 35.5 percent of Chinese Americans, 27 percent of Filipino Americans, 16.7 percent of Asian Indians, 13 percent of Korean Americans, and 4.1 percent of Vietnamese Americans were registered voters in 1984 (Nakanishi 1991). The low voter registration rates among Asian Americans are attributed to many reasons. Some historical and structural barriers to political participation still exist; for example, the splitting of the Asian American population in a given area into several voting districts, and the establishment of at-large election systems in areas with a high Asian American population (Chang 1993). There are also non-structural factors as well, such as the high percentage of foreign-born population among Asian Americans and the general mistrust of the ruling government. Dr. Tran, a Vietnamese American professional, tells me:

I have been a U.S. citizen for 19 years. I have never voted before. I
think that my political line is divided among the two parties. For
Vietnam, the Republican party has maintained strong anti-communist
strategies. But concerning domestic matters, the Democratic party is
much better. That is the rational explanation. My gut feeling is that I
don't feel part of this country. (Interview #60)

If we concentrate entirely on the electoral dimension, we miss
other forms of activism. For one thing, Asian Americans have been a
major source of money for elections but a minor source of votes (Wei
1993). Ethnic churches have also served as centers of social and
political activities. We need to discover the way life in and around
particular ethnic communities helps shape both what people basically
treat as political and, therefore, what should be defined as meaningful
electoral and non-electoral activities. Asian Americans may well have
chosen alternative forms of political action for a variety of ethnically
specific reasons. This would hardly be surprising of people who
conceivably have different senses of what is powerful, effective,
comfortable, and possible. Then what kind of political strategies are
needed and what kind of political activities involve Asians? Steve Kuo
stresses the importance of the grass-root political mobilization in the
Asian American community.

We stayed away from elections. If we go out there and try to
persuade the community to elect someone for the City Council or
District, we get no response at all. Because they don't care about that.
They are concerned about the schools their kids go to, whether their
kids go out in the street and get beaten up. Especially when you're
working with the really disfranchised, they feel that they are not part
of this country. When you're working with those communities, what
you probably have to do is to work outside the system. First of all, if
you're trying to get Asian people elected, an Asian person who has
these resources to get elected probably isn't going to know what it is
like for people who are living in those communities. Good, we get
Asian people elected, but does that mean things are going to improve
for these people? I am not sure. It is difficult to get Asian people
elected in the first place, and even if you do, then how do you make
sure that this person does the right thing? I think one should do things

in a more direct way. Just speak up, make more noise even if you don't vote. We can make change that way too. (Interview #86)

For an upheaval of awareness and political empowerment, education is very critical. Dr. Tran, a Vietnamese American professional, believes that education is the cornerstone of society and a vehicle for empowerment.

> I think that one of the key areas for political empowerment is advocacy of education. People have to be educated more. Unless the whole community realize how politically strong we can be if we stand all together, unless you educate the people up to that level, you are not going to achieve anything. In addition, most of the Asian people are tired of politics. They are still paranoid about government. We should increase awareness first. If we move up to that level, then the vote will count. Unless people see benefits for themselves, people will not do anything. (Interview #60)

However, people in ethnic community are concerned about their homeland politics. There is a continuing involvement of immigrant groups in the affairs of the countries of origin. Competing political parties in the homeland regard the emigrant community as a useful base for organization, and equally homeland governments may be concerned to police such activity and to establish their own organizations. The Chinese government preserves several congressional seats so that an overseas Chinese can participate in the political affairs of Taiwan. The relationship between the home country and the immigration community is very close. To some wealthy Korean American businessmen, becoming an officer in the Korean Association is recognized as a first step towards participating in both American and Korean politics. Quite a few congressmen in Korea have had a previous career as President of the Korean Association in Los Angeles or in New York. There are a lot of instances of raising fund for Korean homeland elections, and frequently Korean politicians visit the United States. Usually many Korean ethnic organizational officers attend such events.

While an ethnic community can become a key political player in negotiating with homeland politics, the focus on the homeland affairs can hinder developing a political ground in the host society. Mr. Cha, a

Korean American social worker, criticizes the excess zeal for participating in Korean politics among Korean American community leaders.

> We, the first generation Korean immigrants, have to be established for the next generation to become successful members of American society. For our political empowerment, I want the leaders of the Korean community to get involved in local politics and to participate in elections. I know that a lot of Korean first generation leaders are much more interested in Korean politics. But what did the Korean government do for the betterment of Koreans in America? We should focus our efforts on the local, and the national agenda in the United States. (Interview #44)

In reality, then, ethnic political organizations cannot be separated from the homeland politics. An obvious reason for the Korean American community is that the Korean ethnic economy is closely linked to the homeland economy. If the Korean economy shrinks, so should shrink the Korean American ethnic economy. Because the Korean American community acts as an important base for the Korean import and export business, Korean American leaders must be constantly attuned to the homeland issues and politics.

SUMMARY

Asian Americans have maintained their identity through language, ethnic holidays and festivals, and numerous ethnic and religious organizations. The ethnic culture they have reproduced in the United States is not necessarily "genuine" or "authentic"—it is contested, redefined, and invented. The ethnic organization is an important mechanism for immigrants to reinforce subgroup differences and a strategy to participate in the political arena.

   With the complex degree of intra-variations in terms of culture and organizational structure, how can we link the diverse experiences in the Asian American community? Anti-Asian violence has been the most important factor for creating a pan-Asian identity. As I have argued before, Asian Americanness is discovered and manifested only after

Asians recognized the similar experiences they had in the United States. Asian is a very broad term to cover at least half a dozen nationality groups of different cultural or religious traditions. Even among the Chinese, Korean, and Vietnamese Americans in Philadelphia, who came from a relatively similar cultural tradition, the solidarity under the same racial term "Asian" requires experiential dimensions. To understand these different traditions I will examine in the next chapter some external ideological dimensions that have constrained and defined Asian experiences in America, regardless of the country of origin.

8
Ideology and Ethnicity

The dominant society presents and espouses cultural values and norms. According to Gramsci (1971), hegemony is constituted and legitimized by a combination of coercion and consent—through education, the media, and religion. It is penetrated into the "common sense of a society," and thus exerts its power at the level of everyday life (Hall 1986). The unequal distribution of material, political and social power is apprehended and rationalized by virtue of group membership; inequalities are thereby ascribed to the intrinsic nature of the groups concerned (Comaroff 1987).

America is a racially organized society, and race is present in every institution, individual, and relationship. Our perceptions and understandings of personal experiences are based on racial categories. The ongoing interpretation of our experience in racial terms "shapes our relations to the institutions and organizations through which we are imbedded in social structure" (Omi and Winant 1994). The state and the legal institution are deeply involved in the organization and interpretation of race.

"White" has been the dominant reference point in the American racial structure. Race is defined from the standpoint of White, thus anyone in America who has even a small proportion of Black ancestry is classified as Black. White racism has been a part of the ideological values of American civilization. The Naturalization Act of 1790— which defines who belongs to the national community—set up criteria for American citizenship as requiring two years of residence and being a free white person. After 1870, with freed Black slaves eligible for naturalization, Asian immigrants became the most significant "other" in terms of the citizenship eligibility. Asians were denied naturalization under the Chinese Exclusion Act of 1882 and the Oriental Exclusion Act of 1924 until 1952 (Takaki 1989).

The racial categorization based on the perspective of Whites, when it is attached with values, becomes the norm. The assumption of White dominance and the racism based on this assumption are systematically institutionalized into the fabric of American society. Father John provides an interesting observation.

> I found a very interesting thing about the Chinese kids. There is a game called "Street Fighter," a very popular video game. In that game, there are probably ten different characters and you would choose one of those people and fight villains. Those characters are multiracial; Asian, Anglo, and Black. All other guys as well as the Asian character are portrayed as fighters. Big white guy looks like Chuck Norris, something like that. Every single Chinese kid, without exception, always chooses to be a big blond White guy. Never do these kids choose Asian. I don't know what that really tells us, but I find it fascinating. I don't think Chinese kids want to be White. But I find something, that those kids have been trained in this culture to see a White person as a model. Caucasian kids sometimes choose to be Asian characters or Black guys. It's interesting that Chinese kids all go for the very same character. I've seen kids play a lot of the times, and they would choose only the one character who is big, White, and blond. Not even White guys with darker hair. (Interview #81)

Our relationships with each other based on the racial formation—both individual and institutional—are so naturally organized that we are seldom made to challenge this cultural assumption. Once the racial classification is fixed, it determines to a great extent our future attitudes towards racial others.

IMAGES AND STEREOTYPES

Stereotypes are sets of traits attributed to social groups. A biological or racial account of characteristics minimizes individual autonomy and individual achievement. Whether negative or positive, stereotypes are essentially false images that obscure the true pictures of complex and diverse Asian American communities. The majority of the stereotypes originally applied to Asian nationals, rather than from Asian Americans, but because most Americans are unable or unwilling to distinguish one from the other, they have been readily transferred to Asian Americans. I will cite some of the lasting stereotypes about Asian Americans. A clear understanding of the stereotypes and their role in perpetuating illusions can contribute to changing those realities.

Foreigner

One of the most enduring stereotypic views of Asians is that they are seen as radically different strangers who have intrinsic foreign features that are not compatible with mainstream American values. Asian Americans are viewed as being Asian nationals or citizens regardless of their citizenship status. Edward Said (1979) has shown that the images of Asians are constructed in the context of the Occidental perception of the "Orient." The Western body of knowledge about Asians, or what Said calls "Orientalism," is a Western style for dominating, restructuring, and having authority over the "Orient." The Orient, according to Said, is an imaginary concept, represented by the West as an opposing concept of the Occident. Referring to Asian Americans as foreigners, then, means Orientalizing Asian immigrants.

The foreigner image attached to Asian Americans invites anti-Asian sentiments and violence. When the nation experiences political and economic crisis, often the blame is directed against the population of foreign origin. The most obvious examples of this kind are the Japanese Relocation during World War II, when two-thirds of 120,000 Japanese Americans who were interned were American-born citizens, and the murder of Vincent Chin, a Chinese-American who was beaten to death by two White autoworkers because they thought the victim was Japanese.

American-born Asian children often receive compliments for speaking English "very well" or even "perfectly." It is a compliment which should cause children to be proud. However, Asian American children are seriously hurt by this "compliment" because it implies that they are not accepted as a legitimate member of American society. The mainstream population's dual expectations of Asian Americans create identity crises. No matter what group they are identified with, Asian Americans are expected to know Asian languages and cultures as well as American English.

Asian Sexuality

The assumed "exotic" origin of Asianness has produced another stereotype of Asians, this time of a the sexual character. In the mainstream media and films, Asian men are often portrayed as being nerd or asexual, and Asian women are presumed to have a submissive character—passive figures who exist to serve men. These stereotypes view individuals as images, not as three-dimensional beings. In the following segment, Melissa is confused by her nature and the stereotype. She questions her boyfriend's interest in her as an Asian woman. She wonders if he found her "exotic" or submissive in any way.

> I knew about the submissive Asian woman stereotype and that Asian women are known for pampering their men. But I never took the next step of realizing that my personality applies very well to that stereotype, and that my White male friend may just see me as "another submissive Asian girl who will do things to make their lives easier." How revolting! I am so shocked at this revelation that I feel stupid for never having realized this before. I hope that my friends know me well enough to appreciate that it is just my personality to be eager to do things for my friends, but again, they may think that I am this way because of my cultural background. (Interview #73)

Although stereotypes are accepted as the assumed characteristics of a certain group, and cannot be indiscriminately applied to anyone in the group, it nevertheless causes individuals to wonder whether or not they conform to the image.

Often these images are internalized in the ethnic population in question. Robert Chun, a second generation Korean American college student, complains about "a sort of introverted type of racism that Asian females often claim that they won't go out with Asian guys because they're geeks" (Interview #63). Being Asian and different from the majority heightens the sense of standing out and leads to the questioning of accepted stereotyped images. Michael Kang, a second generation Korean American, expresses well this reflexive awareness.

> One of my real struggles was with what other people thought of me. I always wondered if I was attractive to white girls or if my being Korean made them not think of me as anything but a friend. I also questioned what my life would have been like had I grown up in Korea—would I have been popular? Would Korean girls have found me attractive? I remember talking with my older sister about these things and she told me that she wondered the same things. That was one of the few times I had ever talked with her about the experience of being an Asian in American society. (Interview #71)

Asians as Malicious Gangs

The image of vicious Asians dates back to the early Chinese immigration to the United States when "tong wars"—conflicts between fraternal organizations for controlling the immigrant underworld—had broken out in many Chinese ghettos around the country. It presumes that there is something sinister about Asians that is beyond the comprehension of Americans.

In recent years the Philadelphia Chinatown and other areas of Vietnamese American communities in Philadelphia have become the site for an increasing number of Asian gangs, and the mainstream media as well as Chinatown residents accused Vietnamese Americans of violence. The gang members include some Chinese Vietnamese and some Amerasians as well. There has also a controversial police practice. The Philadelphia police took random pictures of Asian teenagers, and put those photographs in a mug book (Asian Americans United 1992). Whether they are suspects of crime or not, the police have taken pictures indiscriminately. This is an example of how most non-Asians think of Asians, that "they all look alike." In particular, there is the huge assumption that Southeast Asian kids are villains.

There are many factors contributing to school dropouts and the activities of youth gangs. For the most part, the members of Asian gangs come from disrupted or disturbed homes. Economic hardship forces parents to work long hours away from home; consequently they do not have time for their children. Another factor is that of adjustment without teachers' understanding, positive encouragement and assistance. The effect on the gang youths of incomplete socialization into the two cultures—Vietnamese and American—is a sense of uneasiness in either culture and a reinforced dependence on the peer network (Kendis and Kendis 1976).

Most gangs hang around streets and vandalize neighborhoods, taking advantage of older people, breaking into their houses, and stealing their appliances. Vietnamese people's fear of going to the authorities and their fear of retaliation on the part of the gang members prevent them from confronting this problem. Many Vietnamese and Chinese residents accuse Amerasians of being gang members.

> Most gangs are Amerasians. In Vietnam, Amerasians lived outside the society already. Then suddenly the American government accepted them. Since that time they have became heroes. They had the right to go to the U.S., and for that reason, there have been some unlawful connections. But once they come here, they are neither American nor Vietnamese. They are too old to go to a high school. They become gangsters easily, some organizations recruit them easily. Amerasian kids, they are lonely. Sometimes they live with a single mother. (Interview #51)

Amerasian children were called "gold children" back in Vietnam after the fall of Saigon. People sometimes would buy these kids and use them to come to the United States. But after they arrived in the United States, they abandoned the children. In most of the cases, the family of the Amerasians is a single-parent family. Amerasians seem to be suffering from major discrimination by Vietnamese as well as by Americans. Contrary to what the Amerasians might have thought before they arrived in America, most Americans perceive them as

Vietnamese and not Americans. Some may look more Western in terms of phenotype, but their language, their behavior and their general cultural affiliation bind them with the Vietnamese. Chong Le, who is a social worker at the Department of Social Welfare in the State of Pennsylvania describes the problems of Amerasians. He contends that it is unfair to lump all Amerasians together and accuse them of being gangs.

Amerasians have less education back home because they are mistreated by their own people, and they came to this country with emotional scars. They were hoping to find their fathers, but only 2 percent of them are reunited with their fathers. About 50 percent found their fathers but no further contacts. And they have a hard time dealing with American society. Everything is new to them. Some of them turned to Asian gangs. But there are few cases I know of. Most of them are hard working people. They have family back in Vietnam. They want to help relatives there. My roommate is also an Amerasian. He works twelve hours a day. He sends money to Vietnam to support his family. (Interview #77)

Rather than looking at the Asian gang problem and attributing it to be distinctive in Vietnamese youths, we should look into the way this mechanism is reproduced. Minimal care and attention have been paid to the needs of Southeast Asian refugees in the Philadelphia school system, such as the lack of bilingual staff, inadequately designed English as a Second Language Programs, and indiscriminate age-grade matching (Peters 1988). Truancies and dropouts are not just indications that some Asian Americans are performing poorly in school, having difficulty adjusting, or are simply malcontents. Such behavior may be an attempt to cope with an adverse environment in which the dominant white culture exposes Asians to a broad range of individual and systemic racist practices. In a way, the Vietnamese American gang identity can be viewed as a new strategy providing an acceptable self-image for the youths, as members of a group, on their own terms (Kendis and Kendis 1976). Through this new identity they may attempt to project an image of success to themselves and to others in both the Vietnamese and American cultures.

Asians as Super Achiever

The popular and academic constructions of Asian American children focus on Asian Americans' unique capabilities or "cultural resources" for effective economic achievement: their supposed skill at mathematics, hardworking and frugal habits, and familial economic solidarity. Success among Asian students is portrayed as the result of their inherent or cultural elements. Asian students are constantly used as examples that the American Dream is alive and well and that hard work and ingenuity will always be rewarded.

The ethnic group itself sometimes internalizes the reputation imputed to it by outsiders and uses this as a symbol. In other words, members of the ethnic group themselves may believe the characterizations to be valid, and many Asian Americans use them to represent their strengths. Quite contrary to the strategy of gang youths, scholastic achievement and successes may serve as an affirmation of identity and culture. Whereas some Asian American students withdraw or lash out when faced with overt or subtle racism, others redouble their efforts to excel. This is an example of appropriating ethnicity in a positive way that ethnic cultures defend their cultural values by proposing their compatibility with American goals and values. A 1.5 generation Chinese American school administrator remembers:

> I have experienced the positive effect of the super achiever stereotype. But I must say that I've also experienced the negative aspects of that kind of stereotype. I feel like I've been through most adult life two or three time harder. I had to perform better because I was much more easily spotted. As an Asian American, it's much more harder to be invisible in the White majority world. The model minority stereotype caused me to feel like I really had to do two or three times harder just to keep up. Any mistakes I make really become much more magnified. (Interview #35)

Nevertheless, to portray Asian Americans as super achievers is a false representation, whether or not the content is positive. It depicts Asian Americans in a one-dimensional way, leaving out complexity and diversity in individuals and groups. The majority of Asian American children are not whiz kids. Most of them struggle with language and cultural barriers in school, and often support family businesses after school. The effect of such portrayal, however, is real. If a person does not meet the expectation, the consequences are detrimental. It puts a tremendous burden on Asian American children. I remember one Korean American college student telling me how much he hated those Korean American students who won medals in the Westinghouse competition, and a baccalaureate to be headed for Harvard, and how his parents pressed him so much even though he has been admitted to a decent state college. Moreover, using this apparently positive stereotype as a way to compare other minority groups leads to serious problems.

THE MODEL MINORITY THESIS AND AMERICAN CAPITALISM

The apparent high levels of education, professional occupations, and high incomes attained by Asians in the United States together with relatively stable families and comparatively low rates of crime and deviance have led many scholars and the media to proclaim the success aspect of Asian immigrants to the United States. They have termed Asian Americans as "the model minority," that other races should emulate. However, whether or not the model minority thesis is an accurate representation of Asian Americans, it is not a neutral one. The term "model" directly involves relations with other racial and ethnic groups. Therefore, although the label "model minority" seems like a compliment, in reality it has had a detrimental effect on Asian Americans. It denies the existence of present-day discrimination against Asian Americans and the present-day effects of past discrimination. It also legitimizes the oppression of other racial minorities and poor whites (Chang 1993).

In this sense, the model minority thesis is a racist discourse, which categorizes, evaluates, ranks, and differentiates between groups. Portrayal of Asian Americans as a model minority puts Asians in a position of a racial petite bourgeoisie in the American racial landscape (Palumbo-Liu 1994). Asian Americans are portrayed as a protector of the free market economy, a traditional American value. Asian Americans have accepted the mechanisms and the rhetoric in the

United States that everyone, regardless of color, is rewarded for working hard. By representing Asian Americans as a protector of property, the model minority thesis involves a racially different group, and therefore vindicates the "neutrality" of American capitalism. Asians have been portrayed as "near-whites" or "whiter than whites" even though they experienced and continue to face white racism "like blacks" in educational and occupational barriers and ceilings and in anti-Asian abuse and physical violence (Okihiro 1994).

In the U.S., both popular and academic understandings of race are shaped and defined by the categories of "black" and "white" (Takagi 1993). In this conventional frame of black/white relations, Asian American are perceived to be either like whites or not like whites, or alternatively, like blacks or not like blacks. This peculiar identity of Asian Americans has contributed to the construction of Asian Americans as a "wild card" in racial politics.

Such a popular racial construction has affected the Korean-Black relationship in inner-cities around the country. The construct of conflict defines African American and Korean American identities in opposition to each other. It neatly positions Korean Americans as white, relative to Blacks. Using Koreans as a protector of American individualistic economic ideology creates serious problems however: Korean Americans, not white Americans, became the primary instigators of racism against African Americans. To see this conflict as one between ambitious and selfish Koreans versus lazy Blacks oversimplifies the dynamics of the relationship. Koreans are reacting in anger to having been previously victimized several times and having been struck and knocked down to the ground. Korean business owners are experiencing the frustration of language and cultural barriers, and the emotional scars of downward mobility and the loss of their dignity. African Americans are frustrated because of their long history of subordination both socially and economically in America.

However, the mainstream perspective on this issue has not changed much. During the Los Angeles riot of 1992, national attention was paid to the inner-city Korean merchants and their relationship to African American residents. About half the approximately $770 million in estimated material losses incurred during the Los Angeles riot was sustained by the Korean American community (Kim 1993). Hundreds of Korean shops in South Central Los Angeles were systematically vandalized. While Korean Americans became the targets of violence, their opinions and views were hardly solicited. Without considering the serious injustices and the racism that caused it, the media instead tried to use Korean Americans to sensationalize the situation and to confirm their version of the story, which was about how Blacks and Koreans hate each other, despite the fact that more than half the rioters arrested were Latinos. The stories of conflict construct African American identity in opposition to Korean American identity. "Korean" has been defined in the context of conflict with African Americans. These defined identities invoke a whole set of conclusions that do not follow from a personal or group history or from Korean American or African American experience, but rather from the construction of the conflict in and by media discourse (Ikemoto 1993). The Los Angeles riots or *Sa I Goo* [Korean: April 29, the day of L.A. uprising] had a profound impact on the Korean American community perceptions of their needs. For Korean Americans, the riots raised the important question of what it means to be "Korean American." Like the internment of Japanese Americans, the 1992 riots opened the eyes of Korean immigrants to the problems of institutional racism, social and economic injustice, and the shortcomings of the "American Dream" (Chang 1994).

INSTITUTIONALIZED RACISM

Racism is expressed not just in negative stereotypes but in other forms of preference, through the division and allocation of resources, and through the general maximization of the differences between groups (Wetherel and Potter 1992). Institutionalized discrimination refers to discriminatory acts and policies that are not officially practiced or legally endorsed, but are nevertheless pervasive in major institutions such as schools, banks, and the courts (United States Commission on Civil Rights 1992). A 1988 Philadelphia Human Relations Commission report revealed that while Asians made up under 4 percent of Philadelphia's population, they were the victims in 20 percent of the city's hate crimes. Asians were more likely on a per capita basis to become victims of hate crimes than whites, blacks, Hispanics, or Jews.

An often-cited reason why Asian Americans seldom seek police protection is that Asians are distrustful of the police. Other factors include immigrant Asians' ignorance of their rights under the American judicial system. They feel shame at having become victims and are fearful of retribution by the perpetrators. They are reluctant to undertake the time-consuming and stressful process of dealing with the police at a time when their lives are already complicated by the stresses and strains of adjusting to a new homeland.

Organizations like the police department and the justice system give tacit approval and even foster an atmosphere favorable to anti-Asian violence by their attitude and actions towards Asian Americans in their community. A notable example of this institutional racism can be seen in the David Reilly case (or MaCreesh Playground case) in Philadelphia. David Reilly, a Caucasian youth, was killed in MaCreesh Playground in Southwest Philadelphia after a brawl between White and Vietnamese youths. Steve Kuo, who followed the case from the beginning, described the nature of the case.

> We don't represent people as lawyers, but we've worked with lawyers on different cases involving, like, anti-Asian violence. We put our energy last year on the MaCreesh Playground Case with the DA's office. They [the DA's office] really tried to depict the Vietnamese who are involved as gangs, and believed that these Vietnamese kids conspired to kill the white guy. They tried to get all the people the death sentence. What we wanted to do was to contrast that with how they handled other cases. We're talking about when a Cambodian American man was killed a year earlier. The DA's office knew who the killer was, but they did not arrest the guy for five weeks. We can see that there is a double standard. When the White guy was killed by Asians, all the media got involved . . . For the MaCreesh Case, we met with lawyers from the beginning, we served as a liaison between the families and the lawyers to make sure that they go over all the witnesses they needed to understand. We tried to organize a community protest. We wanted to make sure that the DA's pinned the Vietnamese as vicious gang members. We wanted to get the real story out there, who these guys are, who the families are, things like that. We also wanted to show what the DA is trying to do. Seven young men were involved, six of them were arrested almost at the same time. The other one was arrested a few months later. The DA's office didn't know who did it. All of them were found guilty of

conspiracy. Now they are facing deportation. But the seventh person, that guy was found not guilty of anything. But none of them are gang members. (Interview #86)

A glaring injustice was committed by both the Attorney General's office and the Philadelphia Police department in handling the whole case but especially pertaining to Ty Truong. As a passerby at the crime scene, Ty Truong was fingered by Reilly's friend. He was taken into custody and charged with David Reilly's murder. He told the police that he had gone to a movie at the Cherry Hill Mall. He was identified as being there by his former boss and by the cashier at the movie theater. But the police discounted both witnesses' testimonies by declaring that it was physically possible for Truong to get from New Jersey to Philadelphia in the space of twenty minutes. Only after the police department had gotten other suspects was Truong finally released. At the end of the trial, all six were found guilty of charges ranging from conspiracy to the committing of third degree murder.

CULTURAL CONTENTION IN COURT

The ideal of impartiality suggests that all moral situations should be treated according to the same rules. American courts, in particular, assume a cultural homogeneity for purposes of applying one standard of the law to everyone. However, at the same time, by claiming to provide a standpoint which all subjects can adopt, it denies the difference between subjects. When the instrument for excluding a group is the law, the hurt is magnified, for the law is seen to embody the community's values (Karst 1989).

When identity becomes a legal issue, the legal institution adds another layer of power relationships to the dynamics between majority and minority groups (Minow 1991). Lawyers and judges constitute themselves in the course of defining others. When lawyers and judges neglect the dynamic negotiations over questions of identity, and treat identity as simply something that exists innately and can be uncovered rather than forged or invented, they risk producing not only unfortunate results, but also unconvincing reasons for the results. The use of a specific notion of identity to resolve a legal dispute can obscure the complexity of lived experiences while imposing the force of the state behind the selected notion of identity (Minow 1997).

When judges decide cases, they claim that their results are compelled by the law. But actually, Critical Legal Studies writers argue, that judicial decisions cannot be the self-contained models of reasoning that they pretend to be, but instead, they must rest on grounds outside of formal legal doctrine, grounds which are ultimately political (Tushnet 1991). When the judge and the judged have experienced different processes of acculturation, judicial bias is sometimes unavoidable. The invasion of constitutional rights is least likely to encounter judicial resistance when judges perceive the victims to be markedly different from themselves (Karst 1989). A judge who is raised within the mainstream culture will perceive social reality differently from a defendant who is raised within a subculture. In addition, acculturated differences inhibit the judge's ability to judge fairly when he or she cannot perceive social reality in the same way as does the defendant being judged. The judge, in evaluating the facts of a case and the application and construction of the governing legal doctrine, will interpret them according to his or her own perceptions and not those of the defendant (Lam 1993).

A cultural defense holds that persons socialized in a minority or foreign culture, who regularly conduct themselves in accordance with their own culture's norms, should not be held fully accountable for conduct that violates official United States law, if those individuals' conduct conforms to the prescriptions of their own culture (Norgren and Nanda 1996). Proponents of cultural defense hold that one standard of justice is too rigid to accommodate the experiences of people socialized under different culturally based moralities than those embedded in American law. However, the notion of cultural defense conflicts with the Western legal assumption that all persons are free to make and act upon decisions, limited only by physical coercion or the extremes of mental duress. The majority of courts in the United States have had a hard time accepting cultural defense arguments because they view a major function of the law to be the laying down of a common set of values necessary to maintaining social order. The debate over the cultural defense will be not only about a substantive issue, but also about "how far the United States can go in testing the limits of its social institutions" (Norgren and Nanda 1996).

Examples of contending cultural values and beliefs between immigrant culture and mainstream American culture include spouse abuse—a frequent cultural defense case. For instance, spouse abuse in Korea is often perceived to be not as serious a crime as in the United States on the ground that it is a private affair. Moreover, Koreans think this kind of affair should be resolved at home rather than in court. Other typical cultural defense cases concern the connections between culturally rooted concepts of honor, shame, patriarchy, the treatment of women as property, and gender violence.

The Han Tak Lee case was a simple misunderstanding of two conflicting cultures. Han Tak Lee was convicted for the murder of his daughter in 1989. His daughter was burned to death in a small cabin in the Poconos, Pennsylvania. One of the major reasons Han Tak Lee was suspected was his extremely cold, stoic, and restrained behavior before the coffin of his daughter. Korean community supporters argue that Han Tak Lee was a victim of the language barrier and cultural misunderstanding, contending that a Korean father, being a man, must swallow his pain even at a time of the most extreme sorrow. To American jurors, the act of a husband not hugging and consoling his wife was not understandable. Mr. Lee was convicted of murder with a handful of circumstantial evidence.

A Taiwanese woman Pao-Fong Young's case was similar. She was charged with pouring scalding water over the head of a two-year-old boy in 1989 after the child had been left in her care. Young's failure to get medical treatment for the child's first- and second-degree burns constituted child abuse. Young reportedly contacted Dona Lin, who had taught Young English in Taiwan and whom Young respected most. Being a less educated person with no English, she considered Lin was the only person she could turn to. Upon Lin's absence, Young had to wait until Lin returned her call. Tan, a Chinese American professional who triggered the Chinese community support for Young, said in his statement, "My common sense is different from yours because I have a different educational background, because I grew up in an environment that was different from yours. Do you think your common sense is the same as Mrs. Young?" (*Philadelphia Inquirer* 3/16/93). The defense argued that Young's decision not to seek emergency medical treatment can be explained through differences between American and Taiwanese cultures.

In conclusion, cultural process produces unarticulated assumptions and self-fulfilling expectations about people who are different, and those assumptions and expectations can affect the behavior of legislators and judges alike. A concept of justice that challenges institutionalized domination and oppression should offer a vision of a heterogeneous public that acknowledges and affirms group differences (Young 1990). In order to do so, our attention should be shifted "from the question of identity to the question of who decides any question of identity" (Minow 1991). Such a line of inquiry does not take legal practitioners outside the world of legal principle. Rather, it invites them to seek a fuller understanding of the context in which principle bears on the case at hand (Karst 1989).

SUMMARY

Ethnicity is an adaptive coping tool, and it involves active or creative responses on the part of immigrants. To survive as meaningful units of self-identification ethnic groups must constantly strive to identify and validate the social boundaries which define them. Asian Americans have been struggling against stereotypes. Whether or not these stereotypes are positive, they affect all members of the Asian American community. The state, legal institutions, and the players in these arenas are also active participants in enforcing outside constraints on identity. As a collective identity, Asian American identity, which is imposed and contested, involves different ethnic communities, and thus leads to the creation of common identity.

Part III Reassessing Asian American Identity

9

Conclusion

This book has illustrated the fluidity of American, immigrant, and ethnic identities in Philadelphia and has stressed that these identities are continually constructed and reconstructed on the basis of situationally defined political and class interests. They are not just primordial, nor are they purely voluntary constructions. They interact with outside forces, definitions as well and are important resources for political organizing. A remaining issue is whether these identities facilitate connections or set up barriers.

THE EMERGENCE OF A PAN-ASIAN ETHNICITY

For many years to come, the Asian American community will keep on renewing itself with newly arrived Asians every year. Different Asian American communities will continue to receive fresh faces as examples of what it means to be "Asian." Although American-born Asian Americans will increasingly be employed in professional fields, the ethnic enclave will not cease to exist with new immigrants continuing to arrive in the ethnic communities.

However, Asian Americans have begun gradually to act on a pan-Asian basis facing political and social situations. Despite interethnic and intraethnic differences, Asian Americans as a group have common life experiences favoring the development of a Pan-Asian identity. Moreover, as a racially divided nation, the United States encourages the Asian people the development of pan-Asian consciousness and culture. Each ethnic group continuously uses ethnic symbols to obtain access to social, political, and material resources. In developing pan-ethnicity, each Asian American group de-emphasizes differences and rather focuses on similarities. Although Asian American is an umbrella term, it is also a political resource for Asians who use it to mobilize themselves and respond to the mainstream society. In many ways, the redefinition of Asian Americanness is a reaction to images or stereotypes imposed on Asian Americans by the mainstream.

As Yen Le Espiritu (1993) summarizes, pan-Asian ethnicity derives its consciousness and solidifies it through electoral politics, federal or state funds for social service agencies, census classification, and anti-Asian violence. Not only do Asian Americans consolidate, but they also politicize, using the pan-Asian concept imposed from the outside as their political instrument. Although issues remain concerning the division in the Asian American community between more established Chinese and Japanese Americans and the recent refugees from Vietnam, Laos, and Cambodia, pan-Asian consciousness and movements will continue to emerge.

The pan-Asian movements are more active on college campuses than in the Asian American communities. The common experience of being identified in the same racial group, along with anti-Asian prejudice and discrimination encountered on college campuses, facilitates the development of pan-Asian consciousness. In Philadelphia, Asian American college students at the University of Pennsylvania, Temple, Drexel, have established ethnic clubs and have engaged in a variety of protest movements to protect their common interests. As previously mentioned, the creation of Asian American courses at the University of Pennsylvania was largely the result of student activism.

Comparisons among Asian Americans in Philadelphia showed the internal differentiation within the community, and the position of that community within the host society. An increasingly differentiated "community" makes it difficult to speak of a shared experience, common sensibility, or unified political outlook. However, understanding the heterogeneity—growing multiplicities of race and culture, further complicated by class—in the Asian American community helps to explain how class affects a diverse Asian American experience. Even for the development of a unified pan-Asian ethnicity, the realization of internal differences seems to be essential.

We now realize that race, class, and gender, are not fixed and discrete categories, and they have no self-evident content. They overlap, intersect, and fuse with each other in countless ways. In many respects, race is gendered and gender is racialized (Omi and Winant 1994). In institutional and everyday life, any clear demarcation of specific forms of oppression and difference is constantly being disrupted.

ETHNICITY AS RELATIONS

The study of ethnicity is basically the study of the classification of people (by themselves and others). Human beings classify things all the time. In the course of life, the individual is continually confronted with new situations and new objects and must redefine his or her identity in relation to these objects. Each of us is a unique member of the sets of endless groupings that touch us, be they racial, gender, family, ethnic, or national nature (Minow 1997). The cultural, gender, racial, and ethnic identities of a person are not simply intrinsic to that person, but depend upon that person's self-understanding in conjunction with communal understanding. Relationships between people shape identities which depend on negotiations and interactions between themselves and others.

Therefore, the multifaceted nature of consciousness is not an individual but a collective phenomenon, a consequence of the relationship between "the self" and the ideological discourses which compose the cultural terrain of a society. Social groups reflect the ways that people identify themselves and others, which lead them to associate with some people more than others, and to treat others as different. Groups are identified in relation to one another. Their existence is fluid and often shifting, but nevertheless real (Young 1990).

Rather than identifying a group and looking within its boundaries for its distinctive culture, we now recognize that group boundaries are not "given." The boundaries are socially constructed and situated, and are constantly negotiated; they are multiple and complex. Ethnicity exists, therefore, as a set of relations. As Comaroff (1987) aptly noticed, it is the marking of relations that is "primordial," not the substance of those identities. The emergence of ethnic groups and the awakening of ethnic consciousness are, by contrast, the product of historical processes which structure relations of inequality between discrete social entities.

In theory, all individuals are unique and no one human being is the same as another. However, we constantly distinguish ourselves from others and continue to "cultivate differences" (Lamont and Fournier 1992). The initial identification for differentiation starts from the particular relationship that originally made this happen. In this sense, difference among ourselves is not real; it is not something that exists out there. Difference is constituted by relations. Relation is real; it has always been there. Without "we," there is no "other." More importantly, the concept of "we" implies the concept of the "other."

Identity, then, is shaped by relations. It is the relations which beget the manifestation of identity in different ways. Certain behavioral patterns which we believe to be intrinsic traits or characteristics of a certain group are in fact produced by the relations. What makes identity meaningful depends on the relations and contexts. What holds us together is not some common traits or characteristics but the relations we have. Those traits or characteristics can have different meanings and connotations depending on relations.

When we are to define something, we are lost. That is the assumption of "Being." In a way, we are shifting our thinking from that of "Being" to that of "Becoming"—congruent thinking in many theories in contemporary physics. Is there a such thing, then, as "Asian American?" We can only be certain that there is a relation that has begotten Asian American, and that relation is the key to interpret American society. What makes people feel and act as Asian Americans is not the contents or characters of Asians but the similarity of relationship or contexts which determine their experiences.

At the same time, it is also the relationship that evokes tensions. The question arises, then, as to how we create proper relationships and how we sponsor these relationships. I have argued from the outset that minority experiences can illuminate the essence of American civilization. I will suggest a step further; the minority perspective can reshape our relationships. By boldly taking the minority's position, we can realize the importance of relations that divided us in the first place, and can disentangle the meaning of the differences—assigned categories of inclusion and exclusion based on relations. By challenging and transforming unstated norms based on the existing relations, we can take into account all involved parties that have been begotten by the relations. My study of different Asian American communities is an attempt to realize this end, a step towards the construction of a truly multicultural America.

Appendix I
Interviewees

Chinese Americans (First 11: Taiwan, Next 8: Hong Kong, Next 4: Vietnam, and 1 Malaysia, 1 Mainland)

Interview Number	Sex	Age	Occupation	Education	Generation	Entering Year
35	M	33	Educator	M.A.	1.5th	1968
41	M	35	Newspaper	M.S.	1st	1988
48	M	20	Student	14 yrs.	1.5th	1984
55	F	26	Social Worker	B.A.	1.5th	1984
73	F	23	Student	14 yrs.	2nd	1971
75	M	23	Student	14 yrs.	2nd	1971
82	F	34	Student	B.A.	1st	1991
87	F	49	Architect	M.F.A.	1st	1965
93	F	27	Student	M.A.	1st	1990
94	F	28	Student	M.B.A.	1.5th	1980
95	M	27	Student	M.A.	1st	1990
42	F	27	Student	14 yrs.	1.5th	1986
43	M	35	Student	14 yrs.	1st	1990
46	F	26	Office Worker	B.A.	1.5th	1977
54	M	28	Lawyer	J.D.	3rd	1966
64	F	23	Student	14 yrs.	1st	1991
72	F	24	Student	14 yrs.	2nd	1970
86	M	32	Social Worker	M.S.	1.5th	1967
92	M	62	Office Worker	B.A.	2nd	1932
59	F	26	Hair Designer	12 yrs.	1.5th	1980
68	F	21	Student	14 yrs.	1.5th	1975
80	M	29	Video Store Own	12 yrs.	1.5th	1982

83	M	22	Student	14 yrs.	1.5th	1979
85	M	36	Deli Owner	8 yrs.	1st	1988
88	M	35	Student	M.A.	1st	1988

Korean Americans

Interview Number	Sex	Age	Occupation	Education	Generation	Entering Year
1	M	32	Business	12 yrs.	1st	1988
2	F	32	Cashier	12 yrs.	1st	1984
3	M	52	Jewerler	12 yrs.	1st	1979
4	F	49	Housewife	12 yrs.	1st	1979
5	F	34	Banker	B.A.	1.5th	1981
6	M	57	Gift Shop Own.	B.A.	1st	1971
7	F	56	Deli Owner	B.A.	1st	1964
8	M	36	Clothing Shop	12 yrs.	1st	1985
9	F	49	Hair Stylist	B.A.	1st	1971
10	F	44	Wig Store Own.	12 yrs.	1st	1981
11	F	51	Discount Store	B.A.	1st	1971
12	M	54	Pastor	B.A.	1st	1970
74	M	24	Student	14 yrs.	1.5th	1975
14	M	54	Deli Owner	B.A.	1st	1969
15	M	33	Cashier	12 yrs.	1st	1986
16	M	43	Cashier	12 yrs.	1st	1989
17	M	45	Discount Store	12 yrs.	1st	1986
18	F	47	Jewerlry Store	B.A.	1st	1974
19	M	57	Discount Store	B.A.	1st	1981
20	M	47	Discount Store	B.A.	1st	1978
21	M	52	Laundromat	B.A.	1st	1987
22	M	48	Food Vendor	9 yrs.	1st	1988
23	F	54	Cashier	B.A.	1st	1987
24	M	50	Martial Art Stu.	B.A.	1st	1974
25	F	44	Reg. Nurse	B.A.	1st	1970
26	M	58	Doctor	M.D.	1st	1964
27	F	51	Doctor	M.D.	1st	1966
28	M	48	C.P.A.	M.B.A.	1st	1967
29	M	46	Pharmacist	M.D.	1st	1967
30	M	58	Doctor	M.D.	1st	1965
31	M	51	Restaurant	B.A.	1st	1969
32	F	48	Housewife	B.A.	1st	1966
33	F	41	Clothing Store	B.A.	1st	1980
34	M	59	Engineer	Ph.D.	1st	1974
36	M	70	No	B.A.	1st	1969
37	F	22	Student	14 yrs.	1.5th	1978
40	F	45	Housewife	B.A.	1st	1987
44	M	59	Social Worker	M.A.	1st	1966
47	F	51	Teacher	M.A.	1st	1963
52	F	30	Laundomat	B.A.	1st	1992
56	F	40	Pastor	M.A.	2nd	1958
58	M	23	Student	14 yrs.	1.5th	1976
61	F	23	Student	14 yrs.	1.5th	1976
62	M	23	Student	14 yrs.	1.5th	1975
63	M	24	Student	14 yrs.	1.5th	1975
65	F	65	Grocery Owner	9 yrs.	1st	1959

| 70 | F | 23 | Student | 14 yrs. | 1.5th | 1976 |
| 71 | M | 22 | Student | 14 yrs. | 2nd | 1974 |

Vietnamese Americans

Interview Number	Sex	Age	Occupation	Education	Generation	Entering Year
38	M	61	Social Worker	B.A.	1st	1978
39	M	63	No	12 yrs.	1st	1982
45	F	46	Social Worker	B.A.	1st	1986
49	M	57	Office Worker	B.A.	1st	1990
50	M	55	Pharmacist	M.D.	1st	1975
51	M	58	Restaurant	B.A.	1st	1979
53	M	59	Priest	B.A.	1st	1980
57	M	30	Restaurant	B.A.	1st	1987
60	M	60	Educator	Ph.D.	1st	1975
66	F	50	Grocery Owner	12 yrs.	1st	1978
67	F	22	Student	14 yrs.	1.5th	1980
69	F	23	Student	14 yrs.	1.5th	1978
76	M	44	Engineer	M.A.	1st	1975
77	M	26	Social Worker	B.A.	1.5th	1980
78	M	64	Pastor	B.A.	1st	1975
79	F	35	Hair Stylist	9 yrs.	1st	1982
84	M	50	Priest	B.A.	1st	1989
89	M	28	Social Worker	B.A.	1.5th	1979
90	M	30	Engineer	B.A.	1.5th	1978
91	M	52	Office Worker	B.A.	1st	1982

Non-Asians

Interview Number	Sex	Age	Occupation	Education	Generation	Entering Year
13	F	28	Student	B.A.	N/A	N/A
81	M	35	Priest	B.A.	N/A	N/A
96	M	45	Social Worker	M.A.	N/A	N/A

Appendix II
Interview Schedule

A. Socioeconomic and Demographic Characteristics

Could you please give me the following details about each member of your household, including yourself?

1. Name:
2. Sex and Age:
3. Marital Status:
4. Address (Specify Zip Code) :
5. Have you moved in the last five years? If so, please state old address.
6. Occupation :
7. How many years of formal education has each person had? Where was it?
8. How many of your kin families live in Philadelphia?
9. Who in your family were the original immigrants? Did the whole family come altogether?
10. Where were you and your family from in Korea?
11. Date you arrived in the U.S. (If you were other countries before, please specify) :

Date you arrived in Philadelphia :

Main reason for immigration in general :

Main reason for choosing Philadelphia :

Main source of information :

12. Describe your chances of returning to your country to live in the next 10 years.

13. Under what category did you come to the U.S.?

    (1) As a skilled immigrant

    (2) As a spouse of an immigrant

    (3) As an unmarried child of an immigrant

    (4) As a brother or sister of a naturalized citizen

    (5) As a student or student's spouse

    (6) As a visitor

    (7) Other-Specify

14. Under what category did your spouse come to the U.S? (Give one of the above numbers)

15. What was your English speaking ability when you first arrived in the U.S.?

16. What is your English speaking ability now?

17. How long after you arrived in the U.S. did it take you to find your first job?

18. What kind of work did you do in your first job?

    Were you an employee of a

    (1) private company

    (2) federal, state or local government

    (3) self-employed

    (4) working without pay in a family business

19. What was the source of information that led you to this job?

    (1) Family

    (2) Extended family

    (3) Friend-Korean

    (4) Friend-American

      (5) Private Agency

    (6) Public Agency

    (7) Media

    (8) Minister

    (9) Self

B. Boundary Making and Ethnic Identity

20. Did you speak an ethnic language at home growing up? How much was spoken, where and by whom?

21. Do you speak a language other than English at home now? How often? On what occasions?

22. What was the most common ethnicity in the neighborhood where you grew up?

23. When you were growing up did you consider yourself ethnic (a member of an ethnic group)?

24. Did you grow up in an ethnic neighborhood?

25. Was it important to you or to your parents for you to date someone of your own ethnic group?

26. Did you ever go out with someone who was not from your ethnic group? How about with someone from your ethnic group?

27. What about outside of your religion? Do you think both of these things were equally important to your parents?

28. Did any of your brothers and sisters or aunts or uncles marry outside your ethnic group? How was this seen by the rest of the family? How did they treat them?

29. Would you prefer your children to marry within their ethnicity, religion? race? why?

30. Have there been any specific times you feel you have benefited from being _____?

31. Is there such a thing as a _____-American character? What do you think of when you think of someone as _____-American?

32. Is there any ethnic group you think is close to _____-American? Which one? In what way are they close?

33. Do you think Americans have a stereotype of what being _____-American is? If so, what is it?

34. (Assuming yes to question #33, answer) Is there any validity to it? Where do you think this stereotype comes from?

35. Do you think there ever could be a time when being an American and being an _____ could be in opposition?

36. What ethnic groups are your closest friends from?

37. Do you feel more comfortable being around than non-_____ ? At what times? Any idea why?

38. Do you eat any ethnic foods regularly?

39. Are there any ethnic holidays that you celebrate in a special way ?

40. Do you think your ancestors faced discrimination when they first came here?

41. Are there any nationality or religious groups that you think face discrimination now?

42. Do you think there is an American national character? Do you exhibit those traits? What are they?

43. Have you ever examined any personal discrimination or hostility in getting a house or apartment? Getting a job or promotion? In any other way?

44. What are the traits of _____-Americans that you think are the best, the worst?

45. Tell me briefly impressions about these people whom you might encounter after your arrival to the U.S.

    a. White Americans

    b. African-Americans

    c. Hispanics

    d. other Asian-Americans (specify)

46. I am going to ask you about some people whom you might have ongoing contact with. Could you tell me the ethnic ancestry and religion of all of these people?

    Doctor

    Dentist

    Lawyer

    Clergymen

47. Is there anything distinctive about wedding?

48. Can you describe some of the customs or practices that affect your everyday life?

C. Institutions and Political Process

49. How did you meet people and make friends when you first came to America?

50. How would you compare the friends you have today with the friends you had in your first two years in this country?

51. If you have made new friends since the first two years how did you meet them?

52. Where do you normally socialize with these friends?

53. In the last 6 months have you attended any events organized by an ethnic club or association?

54. Do you sit on any organizing committee of an ethnic association or club?

55. Do any of the friends you referred to before sit on any organizing committee of an ethnic club or association?

56. How many of your present friends are _____?

57. From what source(s) do you derive your financial support now?
    (1) Family
    (2) Friend
    (3) Mutual help organization

58. If you needed to find another job, what source(s) of information would you use?

59. What is your religion? Was it the same religion you belonged to before you came to America? If different, what made you change?

60. About how many days of the week do you estimate that you attend religious services?

61. About how many hours do you devote to the church?

62. Do you hold any position from the church?

63. Please take any formal/informal association that you are currently active.

   (e.g. alumni association, business association, *kye*, etc.)

D. Legal Aspects and Policy Implications

64. Have you ever worked for a political campaign? For whom, what did you do?

65. When you decide who to vote for, does being an ever influence you?

66. How do you expect your children to vote?

67. Would you describe yourself as working class, middle class, or upper class before you came to the U.S.?

68. Would you describe yourself as working class, middle class, or upper class?

69. (as related to question 76) What do you think most are?

70. Do you feel that there exist different groupings within your community? If so, who are they?

71. If you had to finance, a legal, or any other major problem, who would be the first person or organization you might consult with?

71. If you had to finance, a legal, or any other major problem, who would be the first person or organization you might consult with?

72. Have you ever been involved with legal disputes (traffic, divorce, accidents, etc.)?

73. How do you feel your contact with lawyers, police officers, and courtroom has been? Do you think the matter has been fairly resolved? Please tell me in detail.

74. Tell me what you think about "making it" in American society. According to what criteria would, if at all, you claim you have been successful? (e.g., income, education, quality of life, etc.)

References

Alba, Richard D. *Ethnic Identity: The Transformation of Ethnicity in the Lives of Americans of European Ancestry*. New Haven: Yale University Press, 1990.

Alba, Richard and John R. Logan. "Assimilation and Stratification in the Homeownership Patterns of Racial and Ethnic Groups." *International Migration Review* 26:4 (1992): 1314-41.

Aldrich, Howard and Roger Waldinger. "Ethnicity and Entrepreneurship." *Annual Review of Sociology* 16 (August 1990):

Anderson, Elijah. *Streetwise: Race, Class, and Change in an Urban Community*. Chicago: University of Chicago Press, 1990.

Archdeacon, Thomas J. *Becoming American: an Ethnic History*. New York: Free Press, 1983.

Ardener, Shirley. "The Comparative Study of Rotating Credit Associations." *Journal of the Royal Anthropological Institute* 94 (1964): 201-09.

Asian Americans United. "The Asian Mug Book: An Illegal Practice by the Philadelphia Police Department." Unpublished Report. Philadelphia: Asian Americans United, 1992.

193

Bang, Heeduk. "The Self-help/Mutual Aid Component in Small Business within the Korean-American Community." D.S.W. Dissertation, University of Pennsylvania, 1983.

Barkan, Elliott Robert. *Asian and Pacific Islander Migration to the United States: A Model of New Global Patterns.* Westport, CO: Greenwood Press, 1992.

Barringer, Herbert R., Robert W. Gardner, and Michael J. Levin. *Asians and Pacific Islanders in the United States.* New York: Russell Sage Foundation, 1993.

Barth, Fredrik. *Ethnic Groups and Boundaries.* Boston: Little Brown, 1969.

Bentley, G. Carter. "Ethnicity and Practice." *Contemporary Study of Society and History* (1987): 24-55.

Bond, Douglas G. "Study Abroad, Discovery Within: Korean-American Students in Korea." *Korean Culture* 11:1 (Spring 1990): 14-19.

Bourdieu, Pierre. *Outline of a Theory of Practice.* Translated by R. Nice. Cambridge: Cambridge University Press, 1977.

————. *Distinction: A Social Critique of the Judgment of Taste.* Cambridge, MA: Harvard University Press, 1984.

Butcher, Beverly J. "Philadelphia Chinatown Gateway: Tradition Modified." Unpublished Paper, University of Pennsylvania, 1990.

Cabezas, Amado and Gary Kawaguchi. "Empirical Evidence for Continuing Asian American Income Inequality: The Human Capital Model and Labor Market Segmentation." In *Reflections on Shattered Windows: Promise and Prospects for Asian American Studies*, ed. Gary Okihiro, Shirly Hune, Arthur A. Hansen, and John M. Liu. Pullman, WA: Washington State University Press, 1988.

Chan, Sucheng. *Asian Americans: An Interpretive History.* Boston: Twayne Publishers, 1991.

Chang, Edward T. "Korean Community Politics in Los Angeles: The Impact of the Kwangju Uprising." *Amerasia Journal* 14:1 (1988): 51-67.

————. "Korean-Black Conflict in Los Angeles: Perceptions and Realities." In *Koreans in America: Dreams and Realities*, ed. Hyung-chan Kim and Eun-Ho Lee. Seoul: Institute of Korean Studies, 1990.

————. "America's First Multiethnic 'Riots'" In *The State of Asian America: Activism and Resistance in the 1990s.* ed. Karin Aguilar-San Juan. Boston: South End Press, 1994.

Chang, Pao-min. *Beijing, Hanoi, and the Overseas Chinese.* Berkeley: Institute of East Asian Studies, 1982.

Chang, Robert S. "Toward an Asian American Legal Scholarship: Critical Race Theory, Post-Structuralism, and Narrative Space" *California Law Review* 81 (1993): 1241-1323.

Chen, Hsiang-shui. "Chinatown No More: Changing Patterns of Chinese Organization in Queens, New York." Ph.D. Dissertation, City University of New York, 1990.

Chen, Su-chiao. "Language Maintenance and Shift in the Chinese Community of Greater Philadelphia." Ph.D. Dissertation, University of Pennsylvania, 1992.

Choy, Bong-youn. *Koreans in America*. Chicago: Nelson Hall, 1979.

Clifford, James. *The Predicament of Culture: Twentieth-Century Ethnography Literature, and Art*. Cambridge, MA: Harvard University Press, 1988.

Cohen, Abner. "Variables of Ethnicity." In *Ethnic Change*, ed. Charles F. Keyes. Seattle: University of Washington Press, 1981.

Cohen, Anthony P. *The Symbolic Construction of Community*. London: Tavistock, 1985.

Comaroff, John L. "Of Totemism and Ethnicity." *Ethnos* 52:3-4 (1987): 301-23.

Dearman, Marion. "Structure and Function of Religion in the Los Angeles Korean Community: Some Aspects." In *Koreans in Los Angeles*. ed. Eui-Young Yu, Earl H. Phillips, Eun Sik Yang. Los Angeles: Koryo Research Institute, 1982.

Dinnerstein, Leonard and David M. Reimers. *Ethnic America: A History of Immigration and Assimilation*. New York: Dodd, Mead & Company, 1975.

DuBois, Thomas A. "Constructions Construed: The Representation of Southeast Asian Refugees in Academic, Popular, and Adolescent Discourse." *Amerasia Journal* 19:3 (1993): 1-25.

Espiritu, Yen Le. *Asian American Panethnity: Bridging Institutions and Identities*. Philadelphia: Temple University Press, 1993.

Fischer, Michael M. "Ethnicity and the Post-Modern Arts of Memory." In *Writing Culture: The Poetics and Politics of Ethnography*, ed. James Clifford and George E. Marcus. Berkeley: University of California Press, 1986.

Fishman, Claudia Seave. "Vietnamese Families in Philadelphia: An Analysis of Household Food Decisions and the Nutritional Status of Vietnamese Women and Children Living in Philadelphia: 1980-1984." Ph.D. Dissertation, University of Pennsylvania, 1986.

Gans, Herbert J. "Comment: Ethnic Invention and Acculturation, A Bumpy-Line Approach." *Journal of American Ethnic History* (1992): 42-52.

Geertz, Clifford. "The Rotating Credit Association: A 'Middle Rung' in Development." *Economic Development and Cultural Change* 10 (April 1962): 241-63.

Giddens, Anthony. *The Constitution of Society*. Berkeley: University of California Press, 1984.

Goode, Judith and Jo Anne Schneider. *Reshaping Ethnic and Racial Relations in Philadelphia*. Philadelphia: Temple University Press, 1994.

Gordon, Milton. *Assimilation in American Life: The Role of Race, Religion and National Origins*. New York: Oxford University Press, 1964.

Gramsci, Antonio. *Selections from the Prison Notebooks*. Translated by Q. Hoare and G.N. Smith. London: Lawrence and Wishart, 1971.

Habermas, Jurgen. *Communication and the Evolution of Society*. Translated by Thomas McCarthy. Boston: Beacon Press, 1979.

Hall, Stuart. "Gramsci's Relevance for the Study of Race and Ethnicity." *Journal of Communication Inquiry* 10:2 (Summer 1986): 5-27.

Hannerz, Ulf. *Exploring the City: Inquiries Toward an Urban Anthropology*. New York, Columbia University Press, 1989.

Hing, Bill Ong. *Making and Remaking Asian America Through Immigration Policy, 1850-1990*. Stanford: Stanford University Press, 1993.

Hobsbawm, Eric and Terence Ranger, ed. *The Invention of Tradition*. Cambridge: Cambridge University Press, 1983.

Hurh, Won Moo. "The "1.5 Generation": A Paragon of Korean-American Pluralism." *Korean Culture* 11:1 (Spring 1990): 20-31.

Ikemoto, Lisa C. "Traces of the Master Narrative in the Story of African American/Korean American Conflict: How we Constructed "Los Angeles"." *Southern California Law Review* 66 (1993): 1581-1598.

Ishi, Tomoji. "International Linkage and National Class Conflict: The Migration of Korean Nurses to the United States." *Amerasia Journal* 14:1 (1988): 23-50.

Kamm, Henry. "Vietnam's Exodus is Declared Over." *New York Times*, February 17 1994, A7.

Karst, Kenneth L. *Belonging to America: Equal Citizenship and the Constitution*. New Haven: Yale University Press, 1989.

Kendis, Kaoru Oguri and Randall Jay Kendis. "The Street Boy Identity: An Alternate Strategy of Boston's Chinese-Americans." *Urban Anthropology* 9:1 (1976):1-17.

Kennedy, Gerald F. "The Korean Fiscal Kye (Rotating Credit Association)" Ph.D. Dissertation, University of Hawaii, 1973.

Kim, Choong Soon. *Faithful Endurance: An Ethnography of Korean Family Dispersal.* Tucson: The University of Arizona Press, 1988.

Kim, Elaine H. "Home is Where the *Han* Is: A Korean American Perspective on Los Angeles Upheavals." in *Reading Rodney King, Reading Urban Uprising.* ed. Robert Gooding-Williams, New York and London: Routledge, 1993.

Kim, Hyung-chan, ed. *Asian Americans and the Supreme Court: A Documentary History.* New York: Greenwood Press, 1992.

Kim, Kunae. "Rotating Credit Associations among the Korean Immigrant in Los Angeles." M.A. Thesis, University of California at Los Angeles, 1982.

Lam, Anh T. "Culture as a Defense: Preventing Judicial Bias against Asians and Pacific Islanders." *Asian American and Pacific Islands Law Journal* 1:1 (1993): 49-68.

Lamont, Michele and Marcel Fournier, ed. *Cultivating Difference: Symbolic Boundaries and the Making of Inequality.* Chicago: University of Chicago Press, 1992.

Lee, Mary Paik. edited with an introduction by Sucheng Chan. *Quiet Odyssey: A Pioneer Korean Woman in America.* Seattle: University of Washington Press, 1990.

Lesser, Jeff H. "Always "Outsiders": Asians, Naturalization, and the Supreme Court." *Amerasia Journal* 12:1 (1985): 83-100.

Liem, Channing. *Philip Jaisohn: The Fist Korean-American-A Forgotten Hero.* Seoul, Korea: Kyujang Publishing Company, 1984.

Light, Ivan and Edna Bonacich. *Immigrant Entrepreneurs: Koreans in Los Angeles 1965-1982.* Berkeley and Los Angeles: University of California Press, 1988.

Light, Ivan, Jung Kwuon Im, and Deng Zhong. "Korean Rotating Credit Associations in Los Angeles." *Amerasia Journal* 16:1 (1990): 35-54.

Lum, Casey Man Kong. "Communication and Cultural Insularity: The Chinese Immigrant Experience." *Critical Studies in Mass Communication* 8:1 (March 1991): 91-101.

Massey, Douglas S. and Nancy A. Denton. "Residential Segregation of Asian-Origin Groups in U.S. Metropolitan Areas." *Sociology and Social Research* 76:4 (July 1992): 170-77.

Merry, Sally Engle. "Everyday Understanding of the Law in Working-Class America" *American Ethnologist* 13: 253-70, 1986.

Messaris, Paul and Jisuk Woo. "Image vs. "Reality" in Korean-Americans' Responses to Mass-Mediated Depictions of the U.S.A." *Critical Studies in Mass Communications* 8:1 (March 1991): 74-90.

Min, Pyong Gap. "The Structure and Social Functions of Korean Immigrant Churches in the United States." *International Migration Review* 26:4 (1992): 1370-94.

Minow, Martha. *Making All the Difference: Inclusion, Exclusion, and American Law*. Ithaca: Cornell University Press, 1990.

———. "Identities." *Yale Journal of Law and the Humanities* 3 (1991): 97-130.

———. *Not Only for Myself: Identity, Politics, and the Law*. New York: The New Press, 1997.

Moore, Sally Faulk. *Law as Process: An Anthropological Approach*. London: Routledge & Kegan Paul, 1978.

Morawska, Ewa. "The Sociology and Historiography of Immigration." In *Immigration Reconsidered: History, Sociology, Politics*, ed. Yans-Mclaughlin. Oxford: Oxford University Press, 1990.

Myers, Ronald Eugene. "Immigrant Occupational Achievement: A Comparative Case Study of Koreans, Soviet Jews and Vietnamese in the Philadelphia Area." D.S.W. Dissertation, University of Pennsylvania, 1983.

Nader, L., ed. *No Access to Law: Alternatives to the American Judicial System*. New York: Academic, 1980.

Nakanishi, Don T. "Low Registration, Independence Weaken Asian Pacific Vote," *Public Affairs Report* 32:5 (September 1991).

Nishi, Setsuko Matsunaga and Charles Pei Wang. "The Status of Asian Americans in the Health Care Delivery System in New York." *New York State Journal of Medicine* (April 1985): 153-156.

Norgren, Jill and Serena Nanda. *American Cultural Pluralism and Law*. Westport, CT: Praeger, 1996.

Okihiro, Gary. *Margins and Mainstreams: Asians in American History and Culture*. Seattle: University of Washington Press, 1994.

Omi, Michael and Howard Winant. *Racial Formation in the United States: From the 1960s to the 1990s*. Second Edition. New York: Routledge and Kegan Paul, 1994.

Palumbo-Liu, David. "Los Angeles, Asians, and Perverse Ventriloquisms: On the Functions of Asian America in the Recent American Imaginary." *Public Culture* 6:2 (Winter 1994): 365-81.

Park, Jae Hong. "Immigration Inequality: An Analysis of Pre and Post-immigration Class of Korean Immigrants." Ph.D. Dissertation, University of California at Riverside, 1987.

Park, Kyeyoung. "The Korean American Dream: Ideology and Small Business in Queens, New York" Ph.D. Dissertation, City University of New York, 1990.

——————. *The Korean American Dream: Immigrants and Small Business in New York City.* Ithaca: Cornell University Press, 1997.

Peters, Heather A. *A Study of Southeast Asian Youth in Philadelphia.* Institute for the Study of Human Issues, 1988. SSA-RFP-86-0198.

Rabinow, Paul. *Reflections on Fieldwork in Morocco.* Berkeley: University of California Press, 1977.

Said, Edward. *Orientalism.* New York: Vintage, 1979.

Shibutani, Tamotsu and Kian M. Kwan. *Ethnic Stratification: A Comparative Approach.* New York: Macmillan, 1965.

Shin, Eui Hang and Kyung-Sup Chang. "Peripherization of Immigrant Professionals: Korean Physicians in the United States." *International Migration Review* 22:4 (1988): 609-626.

Sin, Eui Hang and Shin-Kap Han. "Korean Immigrant Small Business in Chicago: An Analysis of the Resource Mobilization Processes." *Amerasia Journal* 16 (1990): 39-60.

Shin, Eui Hang and Hyung Park. "An Analysis of Causes of Schisms in Ethnic Churches: The Case of Korean-American Churches." *Sociological Analysis* 49:3 (1988): 234-248.

Sollors, Werner, ed. *The Invention of Ethnicity.* New York: Oxford University Press, 1989.

Somekawa, Ellen. "On the Edge: Southeast Asians in West Philadelphia and the Struggle for Space." Paper presented at the Asian American Studies Conference in San Francisco, CA, 1992.

Spradley, James P. *Ethnographic Interview.* New York: Holt, Rinehart and Winston, 1979.

Suttles, Gerald D. *The Social Order of the Slum.* Chicago: University of Chicago Press, 1968.

Takagi, Dana Y. "Asian American and Racial Politics: A Postmodern Paradox," *Social Justice* 20 (1993): 115-128.

Takaki, Ronald. *Strangers from a Different Shore: A History of Asian Americans*. Boston: Little, Brown & Company, 1989.

Triandis, H.C. "The Self and Social Behavior in Differing Cultural Contexts." *Psychological Review* 96 (1989): 506-520.

Tushnet, Mark. "Critical Legal Studies: A Political History." *The Yale Law Journal* 100 (1991): 1515-44.

Unger, Roberto. *The Critical Legal Studies Movement*. Cambridge, MA: Harvard University Press, 1986.

United States Commission on Civil Rights. *Civil Rights Issues Facing Asian Americans in the 1990s*. Washington DC: United States Commission on Civil Rights, 1992.

Waters, Mary C. *Ethnic Options: Choosing Identities in America*. Berkeley: University of California Press, 1990.

Wei, William. *The Asian American Movement*. Philadelphia: Temple University Press, 1993.

Wetherell, Margaret and Jonathan Potter. *Mapping the Language of Racism: Discourse and the Legitimation of Exploitation*. New York: Columbia University Press, 1992.

Williams, Patricia. *The Alchemy of Race and Rights*. Cambridge, MA: Harvard University Press, 1991.

Wirth, Louis. *Louis Wirth on Cities and Social Life: Selected Papers*. Chicago: University of Chicago Press, 1964.

Wolf, Eric R. "Perilous Ideas: Race, Culture, People." *Current Anthropology* 35:1 (February 1994): 1-12.

Yoon, In-Jin. "The Changing Significance of Ethnic and Class Resources in Immigrant Businesses: The Case of Korean Immigrant Businesses in Chicago." *International Migration Review* 25:2 (1991): 303-331.

Young, Iris Marion. *Justice and the Politics of Difference*. Princeton: Princeton University Press, 1990.

Zhou, Min. *Chinatown: The Socioeconomic Potential of an Urban Enclave*. Philadelphia: Temple University Press, 1992.

Index